The Light Shines Through

Our Stories Are God's Story

CAROLE A. WAGEMAN

Church Publishing
NEW YORK

Unless otherwise noted, the Scripture quotations contained herein are from the New Revised Standard Version Bible, copyright © 1989 by the Division of Christian Education of the National Council of Churches of Christ in the U.S.A. Used by permission. All rights reserved.

Scripture quotations from the book of Psalms, unless otherwise indicated, are from the Book of Common Prayer (New York: Church Publishing, 1979).

"Like a Plumber" by Matt Fitzgerald. Copyright ©2015. Used with permission.

"The New Normal" by Ann Rose. Copyright ©2015 Forward Movement. Used with permission.

"Man in the Bus Terminal" from *The Miracle of Christmas: An Advent Study for Adults* by James W. Moore. Copyright ©2006 by Abingdon Press, a division of the United Methodist Publishing House. Used with permission. All rights reserved.

Church Publishing
19 East 34th Street
New York, NY 10016
www.churchpublishing.org

Cover design by Jennifer Glosser, 2Pug Design
Typeset by Denise Hoff

Library of Congress Cataloging-in-Publication Data

Names: Wageman, Carole A., author.
Title: The light shines through : our stories are God's story /
    Carole A.   Wageman.
Description: New York, NY : Church Publishing, [2017]
Identifiers: LCCN 2016043691 (print) | LCCN 2017003253 (ebook) |
    ISBN 9780819233400 (pbk.) | ISBN 9780819233417 (ebook)
Subjects: LCSH: Bible--Biography. | God (Christianity)--Omnipotence--
    Biblical   teaching. | God (Christianity)--Omnipresence--Biblical teaching.
Classification: LCC BS571 .W28 2017 (print) | LCC BS571 (ebook) |
    DDC 220.95/05--dc23
LC record available at https://lccn.loc.gov/2016043691

Printed in the United States of America

To the glory of God,
whose power at work in each one of us is
more than I ever expected for myself,
and
To my husband, Ed

If God ever gave me a true gift, it was you.

CONTENTS

ACKNOWLEDGMENTS

M Y GRATITUDE TO those who have helped me with this book extends in many directions, and I realize that by naming anyone, I run the risk of leaving someone out. I am grateful for all those who have been part of my journey with God in some way. I don't want to let this moment pass, however, without giving a few "shout-outs" to those who knowingly or unwittingly have been part of the writing of this book.

First of all, to my family, especially my husband, Ed, to whom this book is partially dedicated. You have read and re-read and re-re-read each of these chapters so patiently, faithfully, and skillfully. I am especially grateful (most times) for your calling out the "seminary speak" that occasionally sneaks in and gets in the way of keeping a story real and down to earth.

Our children: Jody, Gavin, and Kate for your love, encouragement, and cheeky sense of slightly irreverent humor in the various gifts you have given me over the years, including my Deluxe Jesus Action Figures (complete with magic hands), my Moses Action Figure, and a treasured T-shirt that reads: "Jesus Is Coming. Look Busy." And, of course, the cherished items you discovered somewhere such as "Last Supper After Dinner Mints," "Atone-mints," and my "Believe in God Instantly Faith Enhancing Breath Spray." Yes, I have kept them all. But my thanks to you especially for your curiosity and attention when I tell a Bible story that you have never heard before using my own style of storytelling. You have been a faithful audience.

Other family members, especially my Mom and Dad who were challenged to begin discovering their own "new normal" at the same time I was writing that chapter. My sister, Diane, for her consistent encouragement along the way.

I also want to acknowledge Keri Toolan, my official "other daughter," who helped me with a photo shoot, and her "bestie" since kindergarten, Jody (and my eldest daughter for real), for the photo editing.

For those in the helping professions, especially, Dr. Bill Levine,

Psy.D., whose spontaneous question, "So, what's between you and God?" provided an important wedge that screeched open a very heavy door I kept securely shut.

In the church realm, my gratitude to many clergy colleagues for helping me articulate and live into my calling as a priest, especially the Reverend David Hall, former rector of Christ Church/Montpelier, Vermont. When I stumbled back into the church in 1998, he was a key link to my pursuing ordination once again. I am also especially grateful to the Vermont Episcopal congregations of Christ Church/ Montpelier, Trinity Church/Shelburne, St. Luke's/Chester, and All Saints/South Burlington, for teaching me, encouraging me, and challenging me to live more deeply into my calling.

Some final "shout-outs" to Paul and Betsy Eschholz for their honest comments that shaped changes to my early manuscript ideas. To the Reverend James Littrell, who kept telling me, "You really need to publish these stories," after hearing them in sermons. To those who have given me permission to tell their stories, especially Darcy, Alyssa, and Holly's family, I am honored to be able to share your unique encounters with God.

I also want to express my thanks to Church Publishing for taking a chance on someone who is a new author. There have been so many of you involved in bringing this work to completion. I am humbled by your expertise and acutely aware of the skills and talents you have shared along the way. I am especially indebted and grateful to my editor, Sharon Ely Pearson, for your guidance, ideas, and encouragement. You always seem to bring a smile to my face and have been terrific to work with. This has been a lot of fun with your tutelage!

Last, but surely not least, I am deeply grateful for the many blessings God has brought into my life . . . of which, Dear Reader, you are one. The best way I know to say thank you to that holy spirit of love is to use those gifts for something bigger than myself. After all, God is ultimately in charge. All we can do is show up, pay attention, and tell the truth. God will take care of the rest.

INTRODUCTION

HE TREASURE TROVE of stories from Scripture provides thought-provoking narratives of people much like you and me connecting with the mystery of God. For me, an encounter with Holy Scripture often feels like a rendezvous with the story of God; the story of God as lived out in human lives.

We might not always think of Holy Scripture in this way, but those ancient writings are an important source of God's story in and among the human creation. We might skim right over them because the stories have become too familiar and we know how they end. In some cases, these stories are too difficult to understand or accept, and offend our sense of fairness, justice, and integrity. It can be tempting to get reactive to a supposed "angry God" rather than consider that perhaps these stories more accurately reflect humankind's "growing up" in understanding Divine Mystery. It is easy to overlook the human drama that is simmering between those two book covers that carry the title "The Holy Bible."

Stories of Scripture matter. They are an important way to understand how God has been working in our lives and in our world. One of the most powerful aspects of these stories, however, is one that is the most overlooked. It is a very simple idea: the people in Scripture didn't know how their story would turn out. They didn't. Just like we do not know how our own stories will turn out.

We frequently slide right over the impact of the human drama playing out in Scripture with conscious or unconscious inner comments of, "Oh, I know that story. I know how it goes." Even perceptive minds shut off to a frequently repeated tale of a human being who is in the middle of a great muddle. After all, each tale turns out a certain way season after season, year after year, ho-hum after ho-hum. Like a well-worn movie, we can even recite the lines without thinking—so the outcome comes as no surprise. That is our loss, for we miss the vicarious experience of entering the story as the main character rather than the observer. We know how these stories turn out because we have the advantage of time and reflection, but the people in the stories didn't know how it would all turn out when they lived it in the actual moment. They faced the same doubts, fears, disruption, and wonder that we face in light of life events that leave us breathless for hope and help. How quickly we breeze right over that viewpoint and fail to grasp how divine participation in the human story is actually what God's story is all about. Our stories *are* God's story.

When young Joseph, son of Jacob, was sitting in the bottom of a pit while his older brothers schemed to sell him into slavery to a passing caravan, I doubt he really knew how it was all going to turn out at the time. Do you think he had any idea he would become Pharaoh's right-hand man and rescue his own family from famine many years later?

When Esther was the queen to King Ahasuerus, did she feel she was between a rock and a hard place upon realizing she was the only soul on earth who could save all the Jewish people from evil and utter destruction?

When Mary, the mother of Jesus, gave birth and breath to a sweet squalling babe, did she ever imagine that one day she would stand at the foot of an instrument of torture and watch his very last gasp?

Did Peter's despair upon denying knowing Jesus after Jesus's arrest lead him to briefly consider the personal choice Judas eventually made? What did it feel like to be forgiven and entrusted with the "keys of the kingdom" even after his heartbreaking and disappointing failure?

Saul was one of the most feared and fierce opponents of the early Christian church. When he watched and approved of the stoning of Stephen, the first Christian martyr, can you imagine his explosive scoff of "No Way" if someone were to suggest that he would one day change his name to Paul and go on to become one of the most powerful and prolific apostles himself?

There is deeper human drama lurking between the lines of Holy Scripture.

These stories are God's story because they disclose very real human drama playing out in ways very similar to our own thousands of years later. Like us, the people in Scripture were living their lives moment to moment. Like us, they didn't know how their story would turn out and, like us, they had the mystery and unknowing out in front and their only choice was how to proceed.

Our own cries of "Oh God, where are you now?" have been angrily thundered and achingly whispered by countless others across the ages. Our own stunned silence when we fall to our spiritual knees in amazement at some mind-blowing coincidence echoes the songs of praise and thanksgiving from ageless lyrics in the book of Psalms. The times when we are humbled to our core mirror the accounts of ancient people who also fell haplessly from grace and still found God waiting patiently for them to return to the Holy One's love. They are stories of ordinary people like us, but they are also narratives that provide the lens through which God's love shines through to the world.

Stained glass windows are masterpieces of art created with bits of colored glass, but they remain expensive assortments of patterns of color until one thing happens—the light shines through. Their beauty is released when the light permeates them. It is God's light radiating through these stories in Scripture that provokes our own faith response. New ways to consider the many facets of our bountiful Creator are stirred and we discover that God is never limited by our own expectations, but always hovers on the cusp of surprise.

Like Moses, sometimes we don't feel quite adequate to the demands of God's call. Like Joseph, adapting and adjusting to his journey's twists and turns becomes a way of life. Like Mary, the mother of Jesus, sometimes our best response to the expanding of God's story in our lives is to collect ourselves and ponder a bit.

Our stories are also God's story if we choose to see them that way. It is through human drama that God works with intricate subtlety and gentle finesse. We might not always see that hand at work, but then again, isn't that part of the mystery? Isn't that part of the discovery when we wake up to the fact that God has not forgotten us but has been quietly at work listening to our yearnings—spoken and unspoken— while providing sustenance in the wilderness of our daily lives?

Our stories *are* God's story. We are living Scripture with all the faults, foibles, and fantastic hopes that our forbearers experienced along the way as well. We are people of a narrative that has traveled seamlessly throughout eons of time. Like a wide river of multiple storylines, scenarios, and intersecting plots running fast and deep, we dip our toes into God's story in this place and time.

Our prayers for guidance, our petitions for help, our acclamations of wonder have all been here before. Yet it does not diminish their importance simply because others have prayed, petitioned, and acclaimed with the same heartfelt entreaties as we. It doesn't matter who prayed what before. Their story was their story with God and mine is, well, mine.

Viewing our own stories through the lens of God's ongoing journey with humankind lifts us up to be part of what God is birthing in us during these days when all seems so hopeless and confusing and unjust. But guess what? God's people have been here before and so has God. And God knows the way forward.

We step into the story of God as we step into this world and travel here for a time. We come, we go, and we leave whatever legacy is ours to leave, but it is the story of God that continues on regardless of whether we are Christian, Jewish, Muslim, Buddhist, Sikh, New Age, or a "Free Range Believer."

Our stories *are* God's story. It is the way in which God seems to keep revealing love and compassion across millennia. "What about all that fire and brimstone?" you ask. Perhaps it is not so much that God is a fire-eating and predictably unpredictable character, but more likely that we are growing up in our understanding of the magnificent complexity of this life-force who creates such a marvelous natural world and yet also seems to be able to pay personal attention to the daily dilemmas of human problems.

I don't understand why or how that works and don't want to get bogged down in theological debates. My interest is to look at the ways in which the ancient human stories of Scripture are God's story and how our stories, too, are part of that ongoing abundance of wonder, grace, and growth.

Themes to Explore

This book is divided into five parts, each focused on a specific theme, with chapters that explore these ideas through the lens of a biblical story. In Part One: God's Storyboard, we rendezvous with the story of God much like an animation production's storyboard that outlines major actions, themes, and situations that unfold in more detail later. Part Two: When Faith and Fear Collide asks the question: What does it mean when an unexpected catastrophe lands in our laps and suddenly we come face-to-face with a faith that just doesn't seem to measure up when we thought it would or expected it should? Part Three: The Bleeding Edge explores how when our heart is broken by life's circumstances and we do not really know what will happen next, sometimes God shows up with new information that is totally outside our expectations and well-laid plans.

God is full of surprises if we pay attention. In Part Four: Letting God Be God, we hear stories about people who had to learn that as well. God is predictably unpredictable.

Part Five: Trusting an Unknown Future to a Known God focuses on the joys, losses, surprises, fears, and opportunities that inevitably shape our lives. While we can't always control those situations, it seems that God works in a discreet partnership with us, creating good and loving outcomes in spite of ourselves.

Using This Book

Each chapter begins with a question posed for you to briefly reflect upon before you begin reading. Next comes a reference to a piece of Scripture that is the portion of Scripture I am exploring in the chapter. You can look up this piece of Scripture in a Bible or on any online source if you choose. You can also refer to the Appendix: Scripture Stories at the back of the book. I have used the New Revised Standard Version (NRSV) translation within each chapter when sharing particular verses to focus on. I have used the Book of Common Prayer (BCP) when sharing particular psalms. You will also discover little comments along the way, inserted onto the page to help you understand a concept or word more fully, or discover a reference to further your study.

As you explore these themes and scriptural stories, you will find some thoughts and questions at the end of each chapter for use individually or in a discussion group. These thoughts and reflections are featured using two different techniques: *Connecting* and *Pondering.*

There are several online websites in which you can read the Bible, looking a passage up by noting the book, chapter, and verse—such as John 3:16. Here are some: Bible Gateway (www.bible-gateway.com), Oremus (http://bible.oremus.org), and Bible Hub (www.biblehub.com). I suggest you select the NRSV as the translation.

Connecting is designed to offer you an experiential opportunity to walk a mile in someone else's shoes; namely, someone from Scripture. Put yourself into the story and let your creativity "fill in the blanks" based on what you might know and also what you might imagine. This is not a test for literal interpretation or strict scriptural accuracy. It is an invitation to have fun with Scripture and see where it takes you emotionally. Live into the character as much as you can. Invent some background details that might be consistent with the culture and geographical setting. Visualize the dusty road and what the grit feels like between your toes. Feel the heat of the sun on your skin and the refreshment of a cool rest under a fragrant broom tree. Imagine your thirst, hunger, and exhaustion after a long day on the road with Jesus and the many crowds. Climb into the character's skin and connect your story with theirs in a personal way as though you were acting out their story on a performance stage. Name his or her feelings, doubts, and hopes. Speak in their voice. Discover the joy that thrills them. Struggle with the murkiness inherent in their doubts and disappointments. Delight in that which amazes them.

As you dig into the story of each character, emotional connections and associations might surface relating to your own life experience. Follow these threads, for that is the point of this exercise. We are not all that much different from the ancient others who have encountered the living God. Discover the connections.

The second reflection opportunity is called *Pondering*, for groups who are more comfortable with a typical discussion format. The questions suggested are not intended to be an exclusive set of subjects for debate. These are a few items aimed at provoking conversation or, in some cases, disagreement in the hopes that the group itself will have further deliberations more in keeping with their own interests.

I hope you will enjoy engaging in this journey with me. These are part of my own story with God because in some ways, perhaps like you, I have walked those paths of call, response, betrayal, loss, shame, restoration, healing, holy coincidence, responding to God's call, trust, and transformation. I have come to understand my story as much more revealing in hindsight than clarity in the moment. As you tune into the stories here, think about your own story and how God is present with you.

"Above all, trust in the slow work of God."[1] Even if God seems to be an unknown to you, the Creator-Being who infuses this world with wonder, amazing marvels of nature, and an unstoppable love that is bigger than death itself takes a personal interest in this human creation. Whether you refer to God as He, She, It, Creator, Holy One, or some phrase of your own liking, my personal experience has convinced me beyond all doubt that God does not forget about us even if we have never come to learn about him or her in traditional ways. So, take heart. God is at work in your story whether you realize it or not.

---

1   Pierre Teilhard de Chardin, "Patient Trust," in *Hearts on Fire: Praying with the Jesuits*, ed. Michael Harter (Chicago: Loyola Press, 2005), 107.

PART ONE

God's Storyboard

Hear my teaching, O my people;
   incline your ears to the words of my mouth.
I will open my mouth in a parable;
   I will declare the mysteries of ancient times.
That which we have heard and known,
   and what our forefathers have told us,
   we will not hide from their children.
We will recount to generations to come
   the praiseworthy deeds and the power of the LORD,
   and the wonderful works he has done. (Ps. 78:1–4, BCP)

God's Storyboard

Engaging with Scripture is a rendezvous with the story of God. Aside from the theological, historical, cultural, and linguistic twists and turns, what we have is really the action of God as lived out with the human creation. In some ways, Scripture is much like an animation production's storyboard where major actions are outlined, themes surface in general ways, and situations gain clarity as the story unfolds.

Scripture is a collection of many stories written across different periods of time, in different cultures, and by different authors. Many of the stories do not relate to each other. Generally speaking, the Holy Bible is made up of sixty-six different books. Thirty-nine of them are in the Hebrew Bible (which Christians call the Old Testament) and twenty-seven are in the New Testament. There are some books that cover historical events while others are more theological reflections.

How many books are in the Bible? There are some differences in this number depending on the Catholic, Orthodox, or Protestant tradition, particularly in which Hebrew writings are included, ranging from sixty-six to eighty-one.

Some works were written by authors who lived close to the time that Jesus did and observed the impact of his life, while others are prophecies that Jesus clearly studied as a young man. Some books contain lovely poetry and wise proverbs while others tell tales of an angry god. Some other accounts are thought by scholars to be stories of total fiction or myths. There are many other writings as well that were not included in the "canon," or final version, of the Bible that was approved for use many years ago. Not all of these books relate to each other either, but they make for interesting study.

In reading the Bible, it is difficult to start on page one and expect you will reach some tidy conclusion to a coherent story by the time you reach the last page. The Bible just does not work like that. Yet the Bible is one of the most popular books according to booksellers; its unique mixture of fact, fiction, fable, and inspiration presents a way to investigate many distinctive ideas about how people understood God in their lives and culture. It is a family album of images, storylines, and history bound together by the loving faithfulness and ongoing mystery of a God that just doesn't quit moving deeper and deeper within the human experience. God has not stopped engaging actively within the lives of his human creation just because some early church fathers put this collection of stories we call the Bible together and called it done. In a very real way, we are Living Scripture—the next chapters of the storyboard that outlines God at work in the world.

In the first two chapters you will discover two threads that frame the idea of Scripture serving as God's storyboard: the theme of covenant and the theme of Jesus as Messiah. All that takes place between God's covenant with his people and the fulfillment of God's dream in Jesus sets the stage for where our own stories fit into the divine dance of God.

CHAPTER 1

The Promise God Just Doesn't Forget

A Story of God's Covenant with Abraham

Reflect: Have you ever received an unfulfilled promise?

Read: Genesis 15:1–6 and 17:1–7

M Y HUSBAND AND I live on the western side of Vermont with the Green Mountains to our east, the Adirondack Mountains of New York State to the west, and Lake Champlain along with the extensive Champlain Valley in the middle. We are far enough away from any large city or town that light pollution does not impact us very much. On clear nights the stars stretch from horizon to horizon and some evenings we can see the Milky Way. I love those quiet moments of standing beneath God's grandeur. In the silence, one phrase from Psalm 8 always rings in my head:

> When I consider your heavens, the work of your fingers, the moon and the stars you have set in their courses, what is man that you should be mindful of him? (Ps. 8:4–5, BCP)

It is humbling to be reminded of the magnificence of creation: the stars, planets, galaxies; the bodies of water and all that swims within them; the many different climate zones and all that survives in them;

and even the creative and mysterious splendor of the tiniest weed seed. In the midst of all that wonder, God just doesn't forget about us. What is humankind that you should be mindful of us and seek us out?

Looking at the stockpile of stars on those dark nights also makes me wonder what our ancient ancestor Abraham must have thought about God's promise to him:

> "Look toward heaven and count the stars, if you are able
> to count them." Then he [God] said to him, "So shall your
> descendants be." (Gen. 15:5)

I imagine Abraham had many such evenings of looking up into the heavens and pondering what God had in mind. Considering that God's covenant was to grant him descendants as many as the stars must have seemed like a pretty impressive promise for someone who, along with his wife, Sarah, was beyond child-bearing years.

Abraham did pretty well as a nomadic traveler. He would have been considered a wealthy and successful man with many possessions and an active household. He was able to defend himself and those for whom he was responsible with trained soldiers, but he was facing a troubling future that he could not seem to fix. He had no offspring. When the day came that he and his wife died, there would be no genetic line to continue on. No one to carry his name; to pass on his story to future generations; to inherit all he worked for in this life; to even remember and honor where

The book of Genesis uses the words "Abram" and "Sarai" in the first covenant promise of chapter fifteen. The second covenant promise found in chapter seventeen is where God changes Abram's name to "Abraham" and Sarai's name to "Sarah." For simplification here, I am using "Abraham" and "Sarah" throughout unless quoting Scripture directly.

Abraham, the faithful forefather of all this promise, was buried. Of what use was all that he had? He did not have that which really mattered to him. At the time of his death, his presence on this earth would be forgotten. In that time and culture, children were an indicator of a healthy relationship with God, so there was a bit of theological quandary here as well as spiritual disappointment in his situation.

God's assurance of "Do not be afraid, Abram. . . . Your reward shall be very great" (Gen. 15:1) did not seem to comfort him at all. What could God possibly give him that would really make a difference in his life? He had no children and even feared that his own servant, Eliezer of Damascus (most likely his chief steward), would wind up being his heir simply by default.

Abraham had already lived a pretty long life with Sarah, but giving birth to their own offspring had eluded them. This one thing, that was more important than anything he possessed, had never come his way and there was nothing he, himself, could do to fix it. It was truly not in his power to create a child of his own just because he wanted it. Yet God tells him to look up to the heavens in the silent night sky. What does he see? Billions of stars stretching from horizon to horizon; his ancestors will be like that, so many he will not be able to count them. How could that be possible?

And then comes a very short, almost throwaway line in the story: "And he believed the LORD . . ." (Gen. 15:6). He simply believed, and God regarded his integrity as honest and upright. So God made a covenant with Abraham that indeed there would be descendants of Abraham's line even if it did not seem so at the time. God's word was more than a promise, more than a personal assurance; it was a covenant.

The idea of "covenant" appears several times in the Old Testament. It is a very ancient and complex understanding that goes back to treaties that ancient societies would make with each other for coexistence. A covenant was typically between two political entities, but throughout the Hebrew Scriptures, it is used to describe a unique understanding of God's relationship with his chosen people, and frequently some kind of "sign" went along with the agreement as a way to mark the pledge. The rainbow in the story of Noah is the sign that marks the covenant between God and all of creation following the Great Flood. In chapter seventeen of Genesis, the sign of covenant is circumcision of all males, symbolizing the singular relationship between God and Abraham and the descendants God promises will follow. Still later in the Moses tradition, the tablets of the Ten Commandments represent the covenant between God and all the Hebrew people who have been rescued out of slavery in Egypt. They eventually put the tablets in a box that they built according to God's specific blueprints so they could carry the commandments with them; it was called the Ark of the Covenant.

For Christians, perhaps the greatest sign of God's covenant with us is found in the life of Jesus, who gave himself fully to God by giving himself fully to us in obedience to God. It is no surprise, then, that Jesus marked that unique relationship by giving us a sign of the "new" covenant with God in the words and ritual offered up in bread and wine during the Last Supper that we continue with today:

> "This is my body that is for you. . . . This cup is the new covenant in my blood." (1 Cor. 11:24, 25)

Covenant is also part of our modern world. In preparing couples for marriage, we talk about the idea of covenant; in their marriage vows, they actually are not promising anything. They are making a covenant with each other, something much deeper than a promise. I can promise to do a lot of things: take out the garbage, call to make an appointment for an oil change, take my vitamins, but in a covenant relationship there is a mutual commitment to be together in some new way that is different from daily expectations. It is a *choice* that is freely made. It transforms the covenant partners from a place of separateness to a place of intimacy and reliance on each other. It is a tie that binds two different pieces together into one new and whole thing. It is a mutual pledge to take care of each other and be faithful with each other that grows into a continually transforming bond of love, devotion, loyalty, forgiveness, and faithfulness. It takes time to live into a covenantal relationship. You don't just take a pill and get it instantly. It needs to be nurtured and is nurturing in return. It grows when tended and stagnates when ignored. It is always there because both parties want it to be so.

We also live in a covenantal relationship with God, even though we are not living in the time of Noah, Abraham, or Moses. And our covenant relationship has the same qualities as those just described: it is a choice that is freely made by God and by ourselves. No one can "make" you a believer. It transforms us from a place of separateness to a place of connection through love, forgiveness, and faithfulness. It is a mutual relationship that needs to be lovingly tended, consistently nurtured, and persistently cherished at all times and through all things.

In the sequence of things, Abraham believed first and then God marked that with a covenant sign. God's faithfulness was never in question nor was God's faithfulness called into being because Abraham asked for a miracle. God's faithfulness was there all along. It came first when God said: "Do not be afraid, Abram, I am your shield" (Gen. 15:1), but Abraham had to make his own choice about trusting God with the unknown and unknowable before God's covenant would mean anything. "The Holy Spirit gate-crashes no one's heart. He waits to be received."[2] The constancy of God's love is there all the time, but we first need to believe that placing ourselves in those hands is where we belong; otherwise we are just looking for a miracle worker to make us feel better temporarily, and what good is that?

It is through those moments of sacred connection and covenant that God weaves the tapestry of our lives and our world. We are honed and purified in our wilderness journeys, whether as a faith community undergoing leadership change or as an individual learning to trust in God's future. God does not leave us to wander alone but walks beside us through all things. That is God's covenant with us and it is worth remembering.

Like Abraham, we have freedom of choice and in spite of the choices we make, God's covenant relationship with us is constant in the signs of love and grace that slip into our world unannounced and unpretentious. Blessings, large and small, are showered upon us through the smallest window of opportunity along the way.

God was already there, waiting for Abraham; God is already here, waiting for each of us. It is the generosity of a God who can't stop loving us and who pours himself out fully without reservation regardless of our ability to be faithful 100 percent of the time. God is wildly, crazy in love with us. All we need to do is to turn to God and God joyously meets us the rest of the way.

Covenant is one of the fundamental aspects of God's storyboard in Scripture. It serves as a foundation for all that comes afterward. God's storyboard continues on through the ins and outs, the successes and failures, the times of war and times of peace, and through the growing up of the People of God as a nation, but also as a people of faith. Eventually, we come to the story of Jesus and his disciples that, for Christians, unwraps God's invitation to be surprised by something new.

Connecting with Abraham or Sarah

Step into Abraham or Sarah's "skin" for a moment. Stand beside them looking at thousands of stars in the dark silent sky. So many stars

---

2   William Barclay, *The Daily Study Bible Series: The Gospel of John, Vol. 2*, rev. ed. (Louisville, KY: Westminster John Knox Press, 1975), 168.

you cannot count them. God has promised, "Look toward heaven and count the stars, if you are able to count them. . . . So shall your descendants be" (Gen. 15:5). There are thousands of pinpricks of light shining within your view, and from this barren and elderly couple will come as many ancestors as those stars. As either Abraham or Sarah, what is going through your mind? What do you wonder about? What has been your greatest joy? Your greatest disappointment? What does it feel like to trust in something that does not seem plausible nor possible, yet God has said it would happen?

Pondering

A storyboard is a sequential group of drawings that outline how a particular story arc will unfold from the beginning of a story through to the end. It is a visual graphic tool used by artists, digital writers, screenwriters, and storytellers to outline the overall direction of a story before production. For our purposes, we are referring to the arc of history within which God has been continually active. Draw your own multiple panel storyboard using one of the suggested options below or something of your own choosing that outlines, for you, what the broad sweep of God's story in Scripture looks like visually.

Option #1: Briefly sketch what you would outline as God's story in Scripture. What stands out as important? What are the major themes that draw you in? What notes would you add in the margins as questions, considerations, or ideas? What questions occur to you that you would like to pursue further? What is missing?

Option #2: Briefly sketch your favorite stories from Scripture. What do the people in those stories have in common? How do you intuit God at work in their life events? What is it that resonates with your own story?

CHAPTER 2

Who Do People Say That I Am?

A Story of Jesus and Peter

Reflect: Who do you believe Jesus is?
Read: Matthew 16:13–24

I HAVE GAINED A greater appreciation for the people in Scripture because in almost every case, the key figures were engaged in some aspect of figuring out where they fit in God's big picture. As mentioned earlier, it is easy to overlook that they didn't know how their stories would turn out. They were just living their lives one day at a time and sometimes moment to moment. The people in the stories of God's big picture had to frequently walk by faith in the dark, not knowing where things were heading yet trusting, or not, that God was in the mix with them.

Trying to keep a focus on the big picture while living day-to-day experiences is especially apparent in the stories of the disciples who are frequently depicted as braving Jesus's "on-the-job" training.

Jesus asked his disciples:

> "Who do people say that the Son of Man is?" And they said, "Some say John the Baptist, but others Elijah, and still others Jeremiah or one of the prophets." He [Jesus] said to them, "But who do you say that I am?" Simon Peter answered, "You are the Messiah, the Son of the Living God." (Matt. 16:13a–16)

Now, Peter is never described as being a disciple who spent much time pondering deep questions, reasoning out well-thought-through observations, or speaking in a carefully crafted narrative. He was a fisherman. He was practical. He called it like he saw it. In his unrehearsed response, he seems to have unexpectedly realized that there had been some deep knowledge in his heart that he suddenly found the words to express: *"You're* the Messiah!" What had finally made its way to Peter's consciousness? In Jesus he saw living proof that God had, indeed, entered into this common and dusty world.

And Jesus knew where this revelation had come from: "Whoa— Blessed are you, Simon son of Jonah! For flesh and blood has not revealed this to you, but my Father in heaven" (Matt. 16:17). And picking up on a question Peter never asks, Jesus tells Simon Peter who he is meant to be as well: "And I tell you, you are Peter [*petras,* the rock], and on this rock I will build my church" (Matt. 16:18a).

It would be on the foundation of the perseverance, persistence, resolve, devotion, and love of flawed, impulsive, doubting, slow-to-understand, very human disciples that Jesus would build the future so that God's light and love might shine in and through them.

For anyone being publically referred to as the "Messiah," however, these were dangerous political and religious waters. It is no wonder Jesus told them not to tell anyone. They were expecting a mighty king, but Jesus was not playing by those rules.

Jesus had some serious reeducating to do with the disciples about what their understanding of the coming of a Messiah should be about.

The people of Israel had been a subjugated people for generations; they had lost hope of ever gaining world prominence again like they had in the ancient days of King David and his son, King Solomon. For a people who deeply believed they were the chosen People of God, it was hard to accept that they might never fulfill what they felt God had called them to be and do in the world. Over time, they had begun to look for divine power to accomplish what human power could not, reading the words the prophets had proclaimed so long ago. The Messiah they were waiting for would be a human sent by God to be God's agent, God's king, to do three things: 1) rebuild or restore the temple in Jerusalem, 2) defeat the enemy that was threatening God's people, and 3) bring God's justice, power, and peace to bear both within Israel and out into the world.[3]

---

3   N. T. Wright, *Mark for Everyone* (Louisville, KY: Westminster John Knox Press, 2004), 108.

But this cosmic shifting would not take place without violence or destruction. For those who lived in the days of Jesus, the idea of a Messiah had one meaning only:

> The Messiah, the Christ, was thought of as a great super-human hero crashing into history to remake the world and in the end, vindicate God's people. Nations would ally themselves against this Champion of God but there would be a total destruction of these hostile powers smashing them into extinction. It was violent, vengeful, nationalistic, and destructive. And finally, on the back of such chaos, horror, and destruction would come the new age of peace and goodness which would last forever. A New Jerusalem would come down from heaven. Jews from all over the world would be gathered together into the new city. All nations would be subdued but it would be a peaceful subjection.[4]

No wonder Jesus wanted them to keep quiet for a while. This over-throw of the natural order, including the destruction of the Romans in particular, is what would have been in the minds of most people who waited for a Messiah, and it is likely that expectation might have been in the minds of the disciples as well. They had already seen Jesus at work bringing miracle after miracle and teaching new ideas that challenged the status quo. The people were responding and beginning to see him as a hopeful sign for deliverance. It made perfect sense. And so, within that context Peter burst out with his "Aha!" moment of *"You're* the Messiah!"

Messiah and **Christ** are the same title. *Messiah* is Hebrew and *Christ* is Greek.

It is against this backdrop of Jewish expectation that Jesus began to download into the minds and hearts of his disciples a very different picture of what was going to be happening next: the Son of man must undergo suffering at the hands of the Jewish religious leaders, be killed, and rise again after three days. Capture, submission, suffering, death—no coming in glory. No power and might. No rallying of the people to get behind him. No destruction of the latest conquerors, the Romans.

It is no surprise, then, that Peter rebukes Jesus, "God forbid it,

---

4   William Barclay, *The New Daily Bible Study Series: The Gospel of Mark* (Louisville, KY: Westminster John Knox Press, 2001), 223–30.

Lord! This must never happen to you" (Matt. 16:22). This was totally in contrast to everything they had grown up believing. It was staggeringly impossible.

Jesus had faced this lure of power already at the beginning of his ministry in the wilderness, yet how persuasive and tempting to hear it again in the voice of someone he loved and cared about deeply. The only response could be: "'Get behind me, Satan.' This is the same temptation I faced in the wilderness, Peter. You are not thinking about divine things but about human things and when you do that, you are not a help to me, but a stumbling block" (Matt. 16:23, paraphrase).

The reeducation of the disciples began with a call for surrender, not strife; for denial of one's self and taking up a cross, not taking up weapons for battle. I doubt the disciples had any clue of how this would all turn out. That understanding would be much, much later when the pieces of the puzzle came together for them. It was yet another time when Jesus turned things upside down and revealed the stretch involved in growing spiritually. If you clutch and hold onto your life as it is, you will really lose that which is life-giving; yet, if you willingly give over whatever it is that you have to honestly give up to follow Jesus's journey, you will actually find an indispensable gift you might not have known was there. Giving over your life is the only way to find it.

This is the call to discipleship, the call into an unknown future. This call of trusting in the darkness is how our storylines and God's storyboard intersect; we don't know how our life stories will turn out either. We can only move forward toward that which is life-giving, trusting in the one who says, "Follow Me."

Benedictine Sister Joan Chittister writes:

> Faith is the willingness to believe that, however dark the present, God's future means only good for us. . . . An alleluia to the future is an alleluia to the courage and faith and effort it will take to wring out of us every last drop of character, every ounce of faith, every trembling "yes" we've ever said to the God of surprises.[5]

God's story continues to evolve in our own time; the covenant remains with us steadfastly faithful and moving forward. Our own

---

5 Joan Chittister and Rowan Williams, *Uncommon Gratitude: Alleluia for All That Is* (St. Paul, MN: Liturgical Press, 2010), 176–80.

personal response to Jesus's calling leads us to become the Living Scripture of our time. We are called to look upon things as they are and seek how God might want them to be. This is not a task for the faint-hearted surely and, if left to our own devices, we run the risk of fulfilling our own desires and calling them to be "of God." That is not what Jesus had in mind.

Jesus always pointed away from himself and toward God—although that did not always go over well with his followers. The disciples had many doubts along the way. They struggled with balancing the world as they knew it with the world as Jesus envisioned it. There is Scripture that indicates some followers left because Jesus's teachings were too hard (John 6:60–66). But sometimes walking in the darkness is exactly what we need to do in order to discover the path that is there.

Common Era (CE) and Before Common Era (BCE) are now widely used in place of AD (**Anno Domini** or "The Year of our LORD") and BC ("Before Christ"). It is felt this new designation is more inclusive of other faith traditions as well as nonfaith traditions such as schools and academic settings.

It is a divine dance upon which we embark when we choose to follow Jesus. With all its mystery, surprise, and provocative ways, it is still a dance that moves with faithful endurance in the story that God is unfolding.

Connecting with Peter

You are Peter, the great fisherman. What was your life like as a real fisherman day by day? Year by year? What did it feel like to be called by Jesus from that hard work into something new, unfamiliar, and for which you might have felt totally unsuited at times? What was it like to leave everything you knew how to do and join him and the others in a life filled with unknowns—new things to learn about yourself and new ways of responding to the needs of the world? Have you ever regretted that impulsive decision? What was it about Jesus that drew you in? What did you yearn for?

While walking down the road, Jesus quietly asked all of you, "Who do people say that I am?" This question got you thinking and wondering. The other disciples burst out with responses quickly: "John the Baptist." "Elijah." "Jeremiah." "One of the other prophets." But you made a different connection and suddenly an idea popped into your head and out of your mouth before you had a chance to think on it further: "*You* are the Christ!" as though a previously elusive something that had been nudging at the edges of your consciousness was now unmasked and starkly visible. From where did that idea come? How did that change your sense of following Jesus?

Pondering

Jesus continually reeducated the disciples to give up the familiar ways they knew in exchange for future paths they didn't know and would have to take on faith. It was a spiritual stretch that moved them into new territory in their personal lives. What spiritual stretch are you encountering in your life experience? What experience of the living God do you yearn for?

PART TWO

When Faith and Fear Collide

I sought the LORD, and he answered me,
   and delivered me out of all my terror.
Look upon him and be radiant,
   and let not your faces be ashamed.
I called in my affliction and the LORD heard me
   and saved me from all my troubles.
The angel of the LORD encompasses those who fear him,
   and he will deliver them.
Taste and see that the LORD is good;
   happy are they who trust in him! (Ps. 34:4–8, BCP)

When Faith and Fear Collide

It was September 11, 2001, when I began my first day of new student orientation at the Episcopal Divinity School in Cambridge, Massachusetts. This was yet the next step in my long journey with God; as a budding second-career priest, I was thrilled to be back in seminary again. While we were doing an introduction exercise, the dean of students came in to the room and said, "Sorry to interrupt, but we just wanted to let everyone know that a plane has struck one of the Twin Towers at the World Trade Center. We will let you know when we learn more." Our reaction was understandably shock and sadness along with prayers for those who might be injured. I imagined something like a small Cessna two-seater that had somehow wandered astray and flown into the side of a really tall building accidentally.

About thirty minutes later, the dean returned and said, "We wanted you to know that a second plane has struck the other tower." A not-so-quiet little voice in my head said, "Uh-oh."

Shortly thereafter, orientation was suspended and everything seemed haywire for a time. The Refectory had a television broadcasting the live events as they were evolving, and we watched the towers on fire, followed by their disintegration, collapsing in on themselves and leaving empty space with columns of smoke where there had been two huge monoliths just moments before. My first reaction was, "Oh. My. God. This is bigger than God. 'They' have won. This is bigger than God." I felt all that I had relied upon for strength suddenly evaporate and the devastating fear that evil had overwhelmed God. What could possibly be left to offer hope?

In the very next instant, I could not believe I was even entertaining the idea that this terrible disaster was bigger than God. As hundreds of souls fled to heaven while the buildings showered down as rubble to the streets below, I was hard-pressed to make a comforting connection between the reality I was living and the spiritual powerhouse I claimed to believe in. Here I was a priest-wannabe, someone who people would look to as a grounded spiritual leader, admitting that my fear was so commanding. It quickly overpowered what I thought was my strong and solid faith.

I did go on to get ordained, but I have never forgotten the day when my faith and fear collided and how quickly one can be humbled by life circumstances. What does it mean when an unexpected catastrophe lands in our laps and suddenly we come face-to-face with a faith that just doesn't seem to measure up when we thought it would? When we expected it should?

Sometimes I have wondered if that is the way our ancestors felt when faced with situations that landed them in the same hot seat of faith. It is comforting to know there have been many good souls who have been down that dark road as well, including those whose stories we hear in Scripture. They surely had their own 9/11 moments, such as when the mighty nation of Israel split into two factions that were eventually conquered first by the Assyrians and later the Babylonians. The leaders and people of significance were marched off into exile, leaving the first temple in Jerusalem behind in ruins. A number of Psalms written during this era reflect the anguish and sense of abandoned grief over their circumstance.

Our faith and fear collisions are not always as dramatic as 9-11 or the Exile; sometimes they come gently in the night as with Nicodemus, a respected Jewish religious leader who yearned to connect with Jesus but wrestled with the leading of his heart and the realities of his powerful public position. Or perhaps these collisions occur like that of a town leader, Jairus, who was desperate to try anything to save his ill daughter, or the story of the unnamed hemorrhaging woman whose desperation for healing had been part of her life for many years. Have you ever wanted to give up? The prophet Elijah experienced such crushing and spiritual exhaustion that he plopped down under a broom tree ready to just give up. "Just let me die here," he bemoaned to God.

Sometimes faith and fear collide when faced with overwhelming odds and societal pressures. The creation of the Golden Calf generated from such a collision, not only of the liberated Hebrew slaves who were afraid, but also of their insecure leader, Aaron, who was also afraid but for different reasons.

Psalm 23 is a reading that is used frequently by people on many different occasions. In light of our nation and the world's global experience with terrorism, ongoing gun violence, refugee flight, and political turmoil, we are clearly in the midst of experiencing what it means to be People of Fear. Shouldn't our story also acknowledge that we are People of Promise as well?

Do faith and fear really collide? All the time. Sometimes in big ways like 9/11 and sometimes in the everyday little decisions we make. That seems to be part of the human condition; however, never knowing how our story will turn out does not mean we cannot learn from those who have come before us and traveled similar roads as we have.

CHAPTER 3

God Leaves No Fingerprints

A Story of Nicodemus

Reflect: When have you stood up for something you have believed in, risking your life and reputation?

Read: John 3:1–10, 7:45–52, and 19:38–42

SOME PARTS OF Vermont are open land and prone to strong winds. When an intense wind blows, it can take down trees, toss outdoor furniture around, down power lines, and blow shingles off the roof as well as impact anything else in its path: crashing, breaking, bending, snapping off, tossing, cleansing. It is humbling to feel helpless in the throes of an enthusiastic wind.

When Jesus says, "The wind blows where it chooses" (John 3:8), he is not just talking about a gentle breeze that comfortably fans us on a hot day. He's talking about a life-altering power that shakes you to your core and reminds you who is ultimately in charge. I don't think Nicodemus had a personal tornado in mind, however, when he snuck out by night seeking to consult with Jesus about what it meant to be "born again."

Nicodemus is specifically mentioned only three short times in John's Gospel, but if we look at those brief story pieces as a whole they are a powerful narrative. First, we need to understand a bit more about who Nicodemus was.

Nicodemus was a Pharisee. This was a "brotherhood" of about six thousand men who pledged to spend their lives observing every detail of the law found in the Hebrew Scripture. The word "Pharisee" means "The Separated One,"[6] and they "separated" themselves from ordinary life in order to study and preserve the many aspects of the law. This was their sacred calling. At some point in his life, Nicodemus had taken this spiritual step. Described as being a leader of the Jews, he most likely was one of the members of the Sanhedrin—the "Supreme Court" of the Jewish community. A pretty select group, the Sanhedrin was comprised of seventy men. They were the religious gatekeepers over every Jewish person in the world, and one of their responsibilities was to deal with people suspected of being false prophets.[7]

In this first introduction of Nicodemus, we know he wanted to keep a low profile in that he came by night. This might have been because he wanted undisturbed and private time with Jesus away from the crowds. It is highly likely, however, that given his spiritual leadership position, he didn't want it publicly known that he was consulting with Jesus. It is interesting that he "plays dumb" with Jesus. The idea of rebirth and re-creation was not a new concept for either Jews or Gentiles, especially for those who spent their lives studying the writings of the ancient prophets.

This first mention of Nicodemus paints a picture of a seeker, but not someone who can really declare himself fully. He stays on the periphery of something that draws him in, yet he is not quite willing to take the next step. He probably understood the metaphor. It is more likely he didn't have the drive to face being "born again" and the life-rattling disruption that it might entail. The thunder of God's presence is merely a persistent whisper that won't go away.

During Jesus's time, a Gentile was a person who was non-Jewish, who sometimes worshipped pagan gods of the Romans or other religious expressions. A faithful Jewish person did not associate with Gentiles and would be considered unclean if they did. This custom was strictly adhered to, which was one reason why Jesus raised eyebrows in his dealings with those considered outside the sphere of the traditional Jewish community.

---

6   William Barclay, *The Daily Study Bible Series: The Gospel of John, Vol. 1,* rev. ed. (Louisville, KY: Westminster John Knox Press, 1975), 121–23.

7   Ibid., 123.

The second time Nicodemus is mentioned is when the Pharisees are having a heated debate about Jesus's questionable popular status as a prophet (possibly the Messiah?) and their inability to get him arrested. Jesus was becoming a problem that had to be dealt with and removed. Nicodemus offers his wisdom and points out to the Pharisees and chief scribes, "Our law does not judge people without first giving them a hearing to find out what they are doing, does it?" (John 7:51). But his colleagues ridicule him: "What's the matter with you—are you from Galilee too? Go back and read your scripture because surely you know no prophet comes from Galilee—that backwater!" (John 7:52, paraphrase).

Nicodemus appears to be trying to give Jesus a fuller audience, but the other Pharisees appear to be intent on an already predetermined direction. Nicodemus slips under the radar again.

As the Gospel proceeds, Jesus keeps teaching, healing, and running up against the Pharisees, who continually challenge him and watch for ways to catch him out. Jesus manages to evade the Pharisees for quite some time but eventually they set a trap, capture him, have him arrested, and put to death.

We can assume Nicodemus was most likely present among the Pharisees in those conversations and as plans were being made for Jesus's capture, or he at least might have suspected what was going on. It is also likely that Nicodemus was present at Jesus's trial. I can't help but wonder what was going on in Nicodemus's thinking and in his heart during this time. How was all this squaring with his experience of Jesus? What seeds of change were growing in Nicodemus's heart as injustice upon injustice was visited upon Jesus? Nicodemus was between a theological rock and a spiritual hard place and the pressure of the Holy Spirit was upon him. Here was this Jesus, a young teacher, obviously living in the presence of and with the blessing of God. Someone who *could* make a difference in Nicodemus's own life but couldn't yet claim it for himself.

The third time Nicodemus is mentioned is after Jesus is dead and still on the cross. Another secret follower, Joseph of Arimathea, has gotten permission from Pilate to remove Jesus's body and put it in a nearby tomb. Nicodemus, who is apparently very wealthy, arrives to help and brings with him one hundred pounds of spices and oils to anoint Jesus's body (John 19:38–42). Think about what one hundred pounds of myrrh and aloe, spices, and fragrant ointments would have looked like and would have cost. Was this a guilt offering too little, too late? Or was this an extravagant gift of love in a moment of extraordinary personal witness?

It is easy to imagine Nicodemus as a somewhat discreet, kind, predictable, and reflective man whose leadership might be taken for granted by his colleagues when suddenly, he is no longer flying under the radar. His actions declare his love for Jesus. He has come out of the closet in full daylight. He has touched and handled a dead corpse, making him unclean on the eve of one of their holiest days, leaving no time to go through the ritual cleansing required. This is not in keeping with the law at all! Such action by this quiet, highly educated, spiritually sharp, politically powerful, community-connected leader within the Jewish community could cost him his reputation, his family relationships, his status in the community, possibly his business connections, and consequently his income. That small still voice of God that had been calling him had caught up with him and thundered through his life; split the flames of injustice that burned in Nicodemus's soul and shook his personal wilderness like a mighty earthquake. He probably was never the same again. William Barclay, a New Testament scholar, points out:

> If a [person] does not wish to be reborn, he will deliber-ately misunderstand what rebirth means. If a [person] does not wish to be changed, he will deliberately shut his eyes and mind and heart to the power which can change him. In the last analysis what is the matter with so many of us is simply the fact that, when Jesus Christ comes with his offer to change us and re-create us, we more or less say: "No thank you: I am quite satisfied with myself as I am, and I don't want to be changed. . . ." It is easy to sit in discussion groups, to sit in a study and to read books, it is easy to dis-cuss the intellectual truth of Christianity; but the essential thing is to experience the power of Christianity. And it is fatally easy to start at the wrong end and to think of Chris-tianity as something to be discussed, not as something to be experienced.[8]

We, God's wandering and wondering children, have much in common with Nicodemus. Nicodemus felt the pull of the Spirit, but he wanted it to be in a neatly wrapped package that wouldn't

---

8 Ibid., 131–33.

be disturbing or messy, one that wouldn't ask too much or be too difficult. He is a lot like us, not necessarily wanting to be changed. We might be curious and even driven, but perhaps not quite prepared yet to take a leap. It might feel safer to stay hidden in the shadows and watch from a distance. Willing to take shots in the dark but not ready to trust the light.

We don't hear about Nicodemus after these three episodes, but how could he not have discovered something astoundingly different in his life? How could he not have become born anew from the Spirit after all? Something of significance was reconciled, leading him into new spiritual and personal territory.

Birth is not something we ask for or plan on. It is something that happens to us when we have gestated long enough in our mother's womb. To be born is to be ready to emerge from one way of living into another way of living so we can grow in the way God intends us to grow. It is a step out of the darkness and finding ourselves surrounded by light.

Jesus was right. You can't see where the wind comes from or where it goes. The only signs that it passed on through are found in the impact left in its wake. The call we experience is from the Spirit around us, but the response comes from the fire within us.

God leaves no fingerprints, but that doesn't mean that this divine source of life is not totally present at all times. God moves quietly and skillfully and with the touch of an angel-whisper. Much like the wind.

Connecting with Nicodemus the Pharisee

Step into Nicodemus's "skin." What has it been like to be part of a religious leadership like the Pharisees who were concerned with maintaining the purity of the Law of Moses? How did you participate in the discussions and decision-making with your fellow religious leaders? Were you one of the conservatives or were you more of a moderate, open to the possibility of considering new ideas? What was it about Jesus that made you curious? What is it you wanted to ask Jesus that prompted you to go out under cover of dark and seek conversation alone? What curiosity continued to grow in your mind in the days and months after that? What role did you play in the decision to arrest Jesus and have him crucified? What pushed you over the edge to "come out" and disclose yourself to be a secret follower of Jesus by helping to claim his body and prepare it for burial?

Pondering

Jesus said, "The wind blows where it chooses, and you hear the sound of it, but you do not know where it comes from or where it goes. So it is with everyone who is born of the Spirit" (John 3:8). What do you think he meant? How was he applying that to his secret conversation with Nicodemus? Describe and discuss some of the qualities of wind. How do they apply to God in your life?

CHAPTER 4

When Faith and Fear Collide

A Story of Jairus and a Story of the Hemorrhaging Woman

Reflect: Have you ever trusted in something you could not see?

Read: Mark 5:21–42

IN THIS GOSPEL reading, both Jairus and the hemorrhaging woman live in the same community. They are probably aware of each other, although they do not travel in the same social circles. Both have reached a critical point of despair for different reasons and face a fork in the road. Whatever decisions they now make will have consequences for the rest of their lives.

Jairus is described as one of the leaders of the synagogue. He most likely was pretty well off, well respected, hung out in powerful and influential circles, and was familiar with the use of power and authority in the community. He has an only child, a daughter who is twelve years old, on the cusp of womanhood. Even though children and women in that day and age were not held in high regard or value, *this* child was very important to Jairus. It would probably be fair to say that she was the sunshine of his life and brought great joy and delight to her father. For some unknown reason, she has fallen gravely ill and is dying. She is in big trouble and Jairus cannot just stand by and easily let her go down to the grave. It is a frantic act of parental despair for Jairus to bolt out the door, possibly missing being with his daughter in her final moments of life, in order to seek out one final thread of hope to save his beloved little girl.

As a member of the community's leadership, he most likely had heard about this Jesus who was gaining a reputation for doing some pretty amazing things. Jesus created a buzz wherever he went and his presence was not always well received. This community's leadership would be wise to keep an eye on him; now here he was in their midst.

In addition to the Gospel of Mark, this story also appears in the Gospels of Matthew and Luke, but it is Luke that gives us this information about Jairus's daughter (Luke 8:41–42).

Jairus is desperate to save his daughter, however, and his back is up against the wall. Things like one's reputation quickly take a backseat when something of real value is threatened. Jairus dashes out into the streets to seek and find this itinerant preacher and healer named Jesus, with the distant and despairing hope that his daughter might be saved from the finality of death.

Jairus finds Jesus. He humiliates himself in front of the entire community by falling to his knees at Jesus's feet and begging him over and over again:

> "My little daughter is at the point of death. Come and lay your hands on her, so that she may be made well, and live." (Mark 5:23)

It was more an act of desperation than an act of faith at this point. Jesus doesn't inquire about this man's motives; he just gets up and goes with him. No questions asked. No explanation necessary. The whole crowd presses in along the dusty street, joining the spectacle in order to see what was going to happen next. This was a human drama and possible miracle emerging right before their eyes. No one wanted to miss it!

In the middle of this jostling crowd, however, there is another human drama quietly unfolding—a woman who has been bleeding internally for twelve years. The same number of years that Jairus's daughter has been alive. But rather than being anyone's beloved, she has been rejected and shunned by her family, friends, and synagogue—the entire community. Whatever meaning she had found in life was long gone due to her physical ailment, for she was considered unclean due to her bleeding. To touch her or to come in contact with anything she touched would make you unclean. Her connection to love, compassion, and caring eroded away years ago along with all of her resources in trying to find a cure. But she had not lost faith that one day she would be restored. That day just never seemed to come.

She did not want to call public attention to her plight the way Jairus did. After being rejected by the community for twelve years, it was just one more potential occasion to publicly become the object of ridicule, scorn, embarrassment, and rejection yet again. But her hope was strong and she felt that if she could just touch the tassel of Jesus's outer cloak that would be sufficient. It would be enough to make her well. She didn't need to be out front and center. She just needed to inconspicuously grasp the hem of his garment.

So in the midst of this mushrooming, jostling crowd, she manages to subtly maneuver herself close enough to Jesus in order to just touch his robe. And everything stops. Jesus turns and looks into the crowd. "Who touched my clothes? Who touched my clothes? Where are you? Someone touched me." The disciples, who are not always quick on the draw, point out, "What are you talking about? You see the crowd pressing in on you. How can you say 'who touched my clothes?'" (Mark 5:30–33, paraphrase). But Jesus knew that something significant

"Every devout Jew wore an outer robe with four tassels on it, one at each corner. These tassels were worn in obedience to the command in Numbers 15:38–40, and they were to signify to others, and to remind the man himself, that the wearer was a member of the chosen People of God. They were the badges of a devout Jew. It was one of these tassels that the woman slipped through the crowd and touched; and, having touched it, she was thrilled to find herself cured."[1]

1 Barclay, *New Daily Study Bible: The Gospel of Mark*, 150.

had happened and he kept looking to figure out who it was, probably still standing close to him, who had reached out with a faith so great that a quiet miracle slid right into their midst and only Jesus and the unknown someone knew. He wasn't going to move until he figured it out. A faith so great is sacred.

So the woman, realizing that her longed-for moment of healing had just arrived, also realized she had been exposed. She came forward in fear and trembling in the middle of all those people. In the deafening silence she fell down before Jesus and told him the whole truth of the matter. And Jesus said, "Daughter, your faith has made you well; go in peace, and be healed of your disease" (Mark 5:34). And she was.

While all this had been going on, however, time had been ticking away. They were no closer to Jairus's house when some people from his household came to tell him, "Your daughter is dead, Jairus. Why trouble the teacher any longer? It is, unfortunately, too late. The mourners have already arrived" (Mark 5:35, paraphrase). Can you imagine what might have been rushing through Jairus's mind at that point? "If only. If only we hadn't been stopped by this woman. If only Jesus hadn't taken the time to talk with her. If only I had sought him out earlier. If only—if only this were not true."

Episcopal priest and author Barbara Brown Taylor says that at this point, Jesus preaches his shortest sermon ever: "Do not fear, only believe" (Mark 5:36). Jairus is asked to take a step of faith: Do not fear. Only believe. Here is a desperate father who refuses to abandon his child to the finality of death. What choice does he have but to step into this unknown territory of trusting in something he could not see? Could not control. Could not understand. Could not measure. Could not influence. He was asked to only believe Jesus and trust in God. Believe Jesus. Trust in God.

This is the crossroads where faith and fear collide. This place where Jesus asks us to put our anxieties, our doubts, and our brokenness on the line and in his hands; to surrender that which keeps us from recognizing that God is always present, always paying attention, always constant, always longing for us to trust just a little bit more than last time. We think we are seeking God in times of our desperation and despair, but how does it turn things around to think that perhaps it is really God who is seeking us? Always.

In my initial interview while pursuing ordination, a priest asked me, "Who do you pray to—the Father, Son, or Holy Spirit?" Yikes! Well, after thinking about it for a minute, I answered, "Well, I think I usually pray to the Spirit but when in times of trouble, I pray to Jesus, but then again, there is that Trinity thing and . . ." He rescued me by saying, "It's a mystery, isn't it?"

I sometimes think about that question and my response because it probably isn't that far off from what all of us do. We go rocking along, everything is going fine—but then something goes wrong. Sudden illness. Unexpected death of a loved one. Broken relationship. Unemployment. Homelessness. Abandonment. "Where is God now?" we cry. "He surely cannot understand the depth of *this* pain. It is too deep for even God!"

Sometimes we march on independently. Sometimes we crash and burn. Eventually we might choose to humbly reach out once again just to touch the tiniest fragment of Jesus's robe in the hopes he might remember us still. But then Jesus turns with a surprised look and says, "Oh, there you are. I'm glad you showed up. I've been waiting for *you* all along."

Scripture scholar William Barclay says:

> No one should need to be driven to Christ by the force of circumstances, and yet many come that way; and, even if it is thus we come, he will never send us away empty.[9]

Well, that sounds great, but sometimes our expectations of God do not quite match up with what God delivers. Sometimes our assumption of what we think God should do blinds us to what God is actually doing.

What about the times when the entire community prays for someone's healing but that person dies anyway? Does God play favorites? What about those who have no community of faith to pray for them? Does that mean God doesn't care about them? Is God a whimsical deity whose actions are predictably unpredictable? Does our personal goodness have anything at all to do with the outpouring of God's abundant grace?

Thankfully, it does not. We are the beloved of God whether we cheat, lie, and steal our way through life or whether we give every last penny of our resources to the poor. God calls us to faithfulness, and each person's path on that journey is different. It is not our job to judge. It is our job to pay attention to our own right relationship with God and then to model that for others by following where he leads, going where he calls, and telling the truth about what we have come to know and experience in Christ. Yet, disappointing things still happen that can cause us to question God's wisdom in what we think is God's promise.

---

9   William Barclay, *The Daily Study Bible Series: The Gospel of John, Vol. 1*, rev. ed. (Louisville, KY: Westminster John Knox Press, 1975), 150, 158.

A few years ago one of my parishioners died of metastatic breast cancer. The entire parish prayed for her healing from the time she was diagnosed a few years earlier until the day she died. She wasn't cured. The cancer marched on relentlessly. Does that mean she wasn't healed? It is important to remember that healing and curing are two different things.

This parishioner was never cured of her cancer, but I believe, beyond the shadow of a doubt, that she was healed of things in her life that had haunted her for a long time. Her gentle presence, persistent courage, and lilting laughter became a healing force in the congregation, something that one might never find in any teaching manual.

She reached out and touched the hem of Jesus. Trusted him unconditionally and he was faithfully present to her through it all: healing her spirit, teaching those around her about grace and love, demonstrating through her life something that went far beyond anything we could have created ourselves. She taught the congregation how to live in the face of death trusting in the joy of God. And at her deathbed, she had the biggest grin on her face because she couldn't wait to join God. It was—she was—pretty special. She was "special" not because of her saintliness but because of her personal response to the same invitation Jesus offered Jairus: Do not fear, only believe. She reached out to touch the hem of Jesus's garment like the hemorrhaging woman and was healed. Not cured, but she got what she needed. With wild abandon and generous abundance, God did not send her away empty but filled her cup until it overflowed.

> The worst human disaster can be met with courage and gallantry when we meet it with God. . . . The great fact of the Christian life is that what looks completely impossible to us is possible with God. What on merely human grounds is far too good to be true, becomes blessedly true when God is there. . . . There is nothing beyond facing, and there is nothing beyond conquest, not even death, when it is faced and conquered in the love of God which is in Christ Jesus our LORD.[10]

---

10 Ibid., 158.

Connecting with the Hemorrhaging Woman

You have remained hidden for so long; it is now terribly embarrassing to be "outed" by the very person you were hoping might not notice your timid hand reaching for the fringe of his robe. Now everybody is looking at you. You are sure everyone can hear your heart pounding in the utterly shocked silence. The town leader, Jairus, is anxious to be off with Jesus to take care of his own desperate needs. You used to walk tall and proud in this town and be respected, but you went from comfort to poverty in an effort to be healed of your bleeding malady. Now shame once again floods your face at being seen so publicly in front of the townspeople who would rather not be near you as though you were a smelly bag of rags walking about on two skinny legs. What does it feel like to have Jesus turn to you alone in the midst of the crowd and love you?

Pondering

We think we are seeking God in times of our desperation and despair, but how does it turn things around to think that perhaps it is really God who is seeking us? In times of personal trouble, where do you turn for help? Do you believe God will really hear your prayer? What is it like to trust that God will be present to you in times of deep despair?

CHAPTER 5

Under the Broom Tree

A Story of Elijah

Reflect: What is it that you need to let die so that something new can be born?

Read: 1 Kings 19:4–8

THE PROPHET ELIJAH was tired. Tired of running. Tired of drama. Tired of being afraid for his life and maybe even a bit tired of serving God. Why are we finding Elijah in a state of exhaustion and spiritual despair? Here is the backstory.

It was a time of great political upheaval and unrest in Israel. They had been in the midst of a three-year drought that had devastated the country. There was severe famine in most of the land. The pagan god, Baal, held sway due to the influence of King Ahab's pagan wife, Queen Jezebel, and Elijah seemed to be the only one left to lift Yahweh's banner high. Perhaps it is more accurate to say that he seemed to be the only one willing to stick his neck out. All the other sacred priests and prophets of the LORD had either been put to death or were in hiding out of fear for their lives. Now, even he, mighty Elijah—widely respected and well known for his prophetic voice, who had totally trusted God in whatever God asked of him—was running from Queen Jezebel, who was hunting him down to kill him. The powerful Phoenician princess was a force to be reckoned with if you crossed her, and Elijah had been a thorn in her side more than once.

Here's how the problem started. Upon Jezebel's marriage to the (Jewish) King Ahab of Israel, the king gave official status to the Baal cult, a pagan religion. Ahab was a rather weak king and Jezebel was a rather brutal and ambitious queen who was intent on seeing that her god, Baal, became the god of the people rather than the One God, Yahweh, who the Israelites currently believed was on their side. God had called Elijah into this precarious and treacherous situation in order to turn the people back to Yahweh, but Jezebel was the kind of woman who would not take "no" for an answer, regardless of one's divine status.

God instructed Elijah to present himself before the king. If Elijah obeyed, God would send rain on the parched land. So Elijah went without reservation. Ahab seemed rather surprised and said, "Is it you, you troubler of Israel?" Elijah replied, "I have not troubled Israel; but you have, and your father's house, because you have forsaken the commandments of the LORD and followed the Baals" (1 Kings 18:17–18). This interchange led to the first reality show contest that has still never been matched: a competition between the gods.

Elijah had Ahab gather all the Israelites along with the 450 prophets of Baal and 400 prophets of the goddess Asherah. Elijah said to the gathered people: "How long will you go limping with two different opinions? If the LORD is God, follow him; but if Baal, then follow him" (1 Kings 18:20–21). The winner of the competition would take all by proving which god was more powerful: Baal or Yahweh. Not only was Elijah's life on the line in case he lost, but the hope of Israel's future was pinned on this one gamble of the spiritual dice, the outcome of which Elijah had no doubt.

Two bulls were brought and slaughtered: one for the prophets of Baal and one for Elijah. Two altars were built and the slaughtered animals placed on them, but they did not light the fire under the offering. Elijah then challenged the prophets of Baal to call on the name of their god to light the fire on their sacrifice.

Asherah was a pagan goddess and considered to be Baal's consort.

The prophets prayed loudly to Baal and ritually danced around the altar for hours. Nothing happened, so their prayers and actions grew more frantic and fervent, even cutting themselves to awaken their god from wherever he was. From morning until noon they carried on but there was no answer. They continued until sunset but Baal never showed up. As a storm god, not only should Baal have been able to send rain to end the drought, but Baal should have been able to supply fire in the form of lightning. The prophets of Baal had failed. They had not been able to rouse Baal from wherever he was cavorting at the time.

Then it was Elijah's turn. He prepared his altar but also lit no fire. He then added to the challenge by having water poured all over the altar and sacrificial offering not once, but three times. There was so much water on Elijah's sacrifice that it swamped the entire thing. Elijah came near to it and said:

> O LORD, God of Abraham, Isaac, and Israel, let it be known this day that you are God in Israel, that I am your servant, and that I have done all these things at your bidding. Answer me, O LORD, answer me, so that this people may know that you, O LORD, are God and that you have turned their hearts back. (1 Kings 18:36–37)

The fire of the LORD fell and consumed the burnt offering, the wood, the stones, the dust, and even evaporated the water that was in the trench. The people fell down on their faces and declared that indeed, the LORD is God. Elijah then ordered all the prophets of Baal to be put to death. God sent the rain that ended the drought as he had promised.

When King Ahab told his queen what had taken place and how all her prophets had been killed, she vowed that this prophet would trouble her no more. She swore vengeance on Elijah and sought to kill him. Running for his life, Elijah escaped into the wilderness and that is where we find him—under a solitary broom tree ready to die himself.

All this time, he totally trusted God in whatever God asked of him or he asked of God. God always came through, so what had happened to shrivel Elijah's soul to the point where he just gave up? Was he physically and emotionally exhausted from channeling the power of God? Was he having his own "Moses Moment" in which he did not feel he was up to the spiritual leadership that God was expecting of him with these fickle and flighty people? We don't know what motivated Elijah's despair, but one thing is clear: he was at the end of his rope, not wanting to go on, just wanting to be done with it all.

His faith and his fear were colliding and he had arrived at an in-between place in his life. Going back was not a good choice and going forward was not all that attractive either. The only thing that was obvious was that Elijah wanted to be done. Elijah had reached that stage of extreme burnout and cynicism that afflicts so many other committed and talented spiritual leaders. Elijah had stopped caring. But God doesn't accost him or shame him or say: "Pull yourself up by your bootstraps and quit whining!" God just cares for Elijah with what he needs. An angel feeds him, tends his body, and gentles his soul.

It is frequently in the in-between time when you can't go back and can't see a way forward that God does some of the best work.

This story resonates with the struggles that so many Christian denominations now experience. Having served God so faithfully, why is it now that everything seems to no longer work in the way it once did? We try harder to repeat those things that worked before, but with limited success. Attaching new ideas to the framework of the old only serves as a temporary distraction from the hard reality that somehow our story has changed and we did not see it coming. Has God forgotten about us? Are we seeking out our own broom tree to sit beneath and wait for the death of the church?

A few years ago, the Reverend Tom Brackett, Officer for Church Planting and Ministry Redevelopment in the Episcopal Church, visited a gathering of the Episcopal Church in Vermont. He had been invited to speak about the massive transitions that are going on in the institutional church, not just for Episcopalians, but for just about every denomination. His presentation was mesmerizing and he spoke of the "in-between" place we seem to be in right now when he asked: "What is God birthing in this in-between place where we are letting go of the past in order to build God's dream of the future? The story we choose to tell will be the story we live into."[11]

As Brackett pointed out, it took the Hebrews forty years to get where they were going once Moses rescued them from slavery in Egypt. Not because they couldn't have traveled faster or because they were lost in the desert. It took them that long to begin to live into the new story of "We are on our way to the Promised Land" rather than the story of "We are only slaves escaping from Egypt."

We become the stories we tell about ourselves. What do we want our story to be? Will our story be about the "good-old glory days," or will our story be about how the People of God eventually wind up under the proverbial broom tree in a state of spiritual exhaustion

---

11 Tom Brackett, Opening Plenary (address, Episcopal Diocese of Vermont Ministry Expo, Randolph, VT, April 21, 2012).

and only then begin to pay attention more carefully to the whisper of God's vision for the future? Surely, if ever there were a time in our world when we need to stop and listen with uncluttered attention, it seems to be now. The challenge of the future is not how to keep our pews filled, but how to survive those things that threaten our very survival: global climate change, income inequality, racial injustice, terrorism, war, political splintering, gun violence, and mass shootings. These are big things that barrage us almost every day.

It is no wonder Elijah got exhaustion of the spirit. He saw those things in his world as well. Big things over which we feel we have no control because they seem so evil and debilitating and we might feel so unprepared. These settings have a chilling effect on our mindsets and outlooks. We become afraid for ourselves, for our loved ones, for our way of life. It is hard to clearly hear the word of God whispering in our ear when anxiety is thundering so much more loudly.

The collision of our own faith and fear is surely not the story we want to live into; however, perhaps that is the story worthy of tackling because we can. It is how God's church of the future might well be evolving. It might well be something God is beginning to birth in this in-between time, when all we know is that the past isn't working all that well but the future is not quite clear yet either.

God might have been birthing something new when thousands of people showed up in demonstrations around the world in late 2002 and early 2003 to proclaim "No" to their leaders before Iraq was invaded. God might be birthing something new in the people who are speaking out against the economic injustices and extreme inequalities in our country. God might be birthing something new in those who attempt to address gun violence in our streets, schools, and movie theaters. God might be birthing something new as we engage with our fear of the refugee whose origins we question. God is surely birthing something new every time someone stands beside someone else who is in trouble and just wanting to melt away under a broom tree.

Like Elijah, we could collapse under the solitary broom tree and say: "I quit. This is too much. I didn't sign up for this. You expect too much from me, God." God would respond: "I know. I know. But I didn't call you because it would be easy. I called you because you would show up. I also know, as do you, how deeply I live within you and how profoundly I love you. You know I am not going away easily. I write this on your heart and put this knowledge into your being. This is the living bread that feeds you, not to assuage physical hunger, but to nourish the longing in you that yearns. I will always be with you as you find a way through the wilderness into a new place."

We belong to God. We are God's people regardless of color, creed, nationality, or faith system. The story we tell of hope, courage, love, faith, commitment, compassion, solidarity, and justice will be the story we become. When we find ourselves hunkered down under a solitary broom tree, it is God who does everything to reach each of us in our individual places of brokenness. In our wilderness we are tended by angels along the way and we, in turn, become the angels who tend others in need.

What new story is God birthing in you? What is it that you need to let die so that something new can be born? That in-between time when the old story is no longer viable, yet the new story has not yet taken shape, is a transition zone rich with possibility. Perhaps it is the only place where real change takes place.[12]

Connecting with Elijah

Have you ever found yourself "under the common broom tree," physically and mentally exhausted, with a shriveled-up soul, "crispy" in spirit, and just wanting to give up? A simple nap under the soothing and fragrant blooms of the broom tree might be refreshing as a stop-gap measure, but there is still the "something more" needed to renew your spirit. If you were Elijah and on the run for your life, what would your soul crave? What would you need from God in that moment? What does God give you?

Pondering

As reflected in this chapter, we become the stories we tell about ourselves. In other words, what we become is shaped by the choices we make, the opportunities we see and pursue, and the hopes we carry. This is true for individuals as well as the church as an institution. What story are you living into? What new story is God birthing in you? What is it that you need to let die so that something new can be born?

---

12 These thoughts stem in part from my reflection on a poem by Danaan Parry, "Fear of Transformation," www.earthstewards.org/ESN-Trapeze.asp, accessed April 12, 2012.

CHAPTER 6

Do You Know God's First Name?

A Story of Aaron and the Golden Calf

Reflect: When have you found yourself in an in-between time, a time caught between the old and the new?

Read: Exodus 32:1–6

A FEW YEARS AGO, my husband, Ed, said he had been privileged to discover God's first name. I said, "Okay. Tell me. What *is* God's first name?" He said: "God's first name is 'O.'"

O? Oh. Oh, I get it. "Oh! God!"

Now that is one prayer that might well be the most petitioned prayer ever: "Oh God—where are you now?" That straightforward plea from the human heart has been wept, howled, thundered, wailed, and whispered since the beginning of humankind during times of trouble.

The divine response to that cry is often a mystery. The human response to that cry varies. There are very few who are able to actually embrace the spiritual stretch of waiting in the wilderness and trusting that God has heard and will respond. Most of us swing from hiding our wounds (as though God won't notice if we bury our heads in the sand) to a place of cynicism and despair when answers don't appear immediately in our time frame or when an answer comes that isn't the one desired. It is a great temptation to say, "God doesn't hear me, so therefore prayer doesn't work."

Some, like the frustrated Hebrew people in Exodus, take matters into their own hands and confront whatever or whoever is in front of them to fix things so they might feel better.

"Oh God—where are you now?" might well have been what went through Aaron's mind as he was surrounded by the fractious, fearful, and demanding former Egyptian slaves who wanted answers and action. Can you blame them? Moses had been gone a long time back up on the mountain. The people responded the way most people would. They began to get restless and anxious in this uncertain time. Insecurity was rising and they wondered: "Why hasn't he returned yet? Is he ever coming back? Did he fall into a crevasse and is lying somewhere injured? Has he been eaten by a mountain lion? What if— what if he *never* comes back and we are just stuck here *forever*? What then?"

Poor Aaron. Brother of Moses. Faithful servant. Called by God to partner with Moses as his spokesperson during the entire quest of confronting the mighty Pharaoh of Egypt. Aaron did well when given instructions, but did not have the commanding presence and respect that Moses had in the eyes of the people. Yet here he was left in charge while Moses continued to collect God's instructions for the people up on the holy mountain. When Moses did not return quickly, the anxiety of the people bubbled over and all they wanted to know was what Aaron was going to do about it. Aaron might well have been pondering the same questions that these former slaves were asking: "What am I going to do now? O God, where are you *now*?"

What an amazing leadership triangle: Aaron. The People. The Anxiety. Here he was: one person standing alone, slightly adrift without a sail, rudder, or even a leaky boat. His faith had always been strengthened by Moses's commanding presence, but in this circumstance, his spiritual courage was jarred by the fear that he was left alone to handle an impossible situation.

Aaron could be resourceful, however, so he lessened everyone's anxiety by giving the people what they thought they needed. He allowed them to turn to old familiar customs as a way to be comforted. At his command, they took all the jewelry that had been given to them when they left Egypt, melted it down, and made an idol: a golden calf. Aaron even added an altar that provided a touchstone of familiarity. This was something that could be seen and transported and around which the people danced, sang, and worshiped. No more of this invisible God stuff for them. The ways of the past were good enough for them before; they might be good enough for them now.

When faith and fear collide, it is tempting to grasp at whatever comes along first that offers comfort, assurance, and confidence; however, sometimes the most powerful spiritual moments are found in the most unsettling circumstances.

While the people might have felt they were helpless and things were hopeless, they were neither stranded nor were they without possibility. They were in the middle of an in-between space much like any faith community might find itself from time to time. Instead of moving forward into the unknown, they tried to remain in the familiar, which really had the ultimate effect of keeping them stuck. It is one of those "inconvenient truths" that "people grow through challenge and not by simply being made to feel better about their plight."[13]

It would not be surprising if this strikes a chord with some readers. Seismic shifts in the traditional "church" make everyone a bit nervous about the future these days. Will there be enough people so there will be enough money so we can keep the lights on and everything will stay the way we like it? Basically, we are an uncomfortable bunch of God's people traveling in our own wilderness and we want some assurance God has not forgotten where we are.

The lessons present in ancient tales such as the golden calf story in Exodus offers us wisdom for our own situation in the church today:

> Biblical stories remind us that the people of God are a people on a journey often living through in-between times. When they failed to create sacred time and space, our biblical ancestors found it difficult to focus on God's leading, God's providing, and God's calling them to a specific purpose in that specific moment. Just as God calls each believer into a life of love and witness, so too does God call each congregation. That call might express itself a certain way for years; but eventually the circumstances that gave rise to a particular church will change. This community of faith may find itself wondering how to get back to the "good ol' days." But God's invitation to congregations facing these

---

13 David W. Cox, "The Edwin Friedman Model of Family Systems Thinking: Lessons For Organizational Leaders" (Jonesboro: Arkansas State University, 2006).

in-between times is more challenging—yet also more faith-filled. God invites congregations to imagine how their own past might influence God's call today and into the future. . . . When things are rocking along as usual, it's easy to forget that we are not just another group of people who happen to get together on Sundays. We are a people called by God— and God has a purpose for us."[14]

The Hebrew people were in a transition space, uncomfortable for sure. If we step away and look at this from a thirty-thousand-foot perspective, we see they were in the middle of God's story that was unfolding as they went along. It felt like bitter wilderness to them at the time. They did not know how it would all turn out.

Those transition spaces are moments of grace if we choose to see them as such. The question: *"Oh God, where are you now?"* is perhaps not really a question of where God is, but where we are in our understanding and ability to stand with courage and integrity during the in-between times.

Perhaps this unsettled time in our own history provides an opportunity, albeit a demanding one, to practice what we say we believe. In God's kingdom, all things work for good. We can remember that in the middle of our muddle, it is the natural cycle of life that we die to one thing in order to rise to something new.

The Hebrew people had to die to their old life of slavery in order to rise to their new identity as the People of God. In the New Testament stories, Jesus's disciples had to die to their old lives as admirers of Jesus and rise to their new call as ambassadors of God's Good News. Even the political and financial shifting within traditionally secure mainline churches are the same processes of something dying and something new being born.

Like the newly freed Hebrew slaves dancing around a golden calf, we don't change anything if we cling to the idols that are most familiar to us. And idols can be tricky to identify sometimes.

In a daily devotional written by the Reverend Martin B. Copenhaver, there are four questions he suggests we ask ourselves if we want to know what our idols are: Where is your ultimate loyalty? What do you consistently make time for? In what have you put your trust?

---

14 Beverly A. Thompson and George B. Thompson, "Finding Yourself in the In-Between," *Alban Weekly* Issue #374 (September 26, 2011), https://alban.org/archive/finding-yourself-in-the-in-between/.

Where can you be most deeply threatened?[15] The fourth question is the most penetrating question because that is what we protect out of fear. Sometimes the things we try to protect take the place of God. Not always, but sometimes.

We all have idols of one sort or another and sometimes they might even be good things. They still rob us of some key spiritual promise, however, when we invest our fullest energy and ultimate allegiance in those things rather than in the one true God. So, if you are disappointed in God's performance lately, it might be because there is an idol or two hanging around that you have not even realized is there.

Sometimes that feels a lot like wandering in the wilderness and being tempted to create a golden calf to relieve the anxiety. Sometimes it is easier to complain rather than seek out the new story God might be creating right in front of us.

There is only one God who wanders with us through the wilderness. There is only one God who asks us to trust in his light when we are in darkness. There is only one God who never forgets where we are, who we are, and who we have been created to be, regardless of our spiritual wandering into an unknown future.

Connecting with Aaron

Welcome to the "Aaron's Wilderness Experience." You have been temporarily placed in a leadership position with a large, fractious group of people wanting answers, direction, and action. Your job was to maintain the status quo until the real leader, Moses, came back. You have no idea where he is, nor when he is going to show up. Day after day you have been waiting and people are growing restless. Rumor has started to spread in the camp that Moses has abandoned everyone and left them because the job was just too much for him. It doesn't help that the gossipmongers are having a field day with the situation. Now nothing is working. They are ready to revolt and you have no answers. How can you buy some time? Why has God gone silent? What are you going to do now?

What does it feel like to be Aaron at this moment in time? Fear? Frustration? Resignation about giving the people something to pacify them? Offering that which is familiar is a tantalizing tease to quell the disturbance. What does it feel like to be manipulated by the

---

15 Martin B. Copenhaver, "Stillspeaking Daily Devotional: Finding God in All the Wrong Places," September 21, 2011, www.ucc.org/daily_devotional.

situation? What other options could you try? Do you think God really knows or cares about what is going on in the camp?

Pondering

Reflect on the four questions suggested by the Rev. Martin B. Copenhaver regarding discovering what our idols are:

- Where is your ultimate loyalty?
- What do you consistently make time for?
- In what have you put your trust?
- Where can you be most deeply threatened?

CHAPTER 7

People of Fear— People of Promise

A Story of the Good Shepherd

Reflect: Where do you turn when your faith collides with your fears?

Read: Psalm 23

I N THE SUMMER of 2012, I spent one week as a chaplain for youngsters ages ten to thirteen at the Diocese of Vermont's annual Rockpoint Summer Camp Conferences. We worked with twenty-nine youth that week with our experiential theme: "Respecting Water—Protecting Water." Camp songs, s'mores, regular worship throughout the day, games, swimming, and all those other fun things that go into a successful and memorable summer camp for kids were fully included. It was a wonderful week that had a jarring end for the leaders when, shortly before we began our concluding Friday session, we heard the breaking news of shootings in a movie theater at the opening of a new Batman movie in Aurora, Colorado. We didn't share that news with the campers, of course, but it was an emotional disconnect to be in this wildly beautiful and serene place with such promising young people, while at the same time, this story of carnage and the deaths of other young people was unfolding elsewhere in our country.

Tragedy such as this brings us up short against our mortality as we again ask ourselves those riveting questions: How can this happen here? How could God let this happen? Is this God's will for those people who died or were wounded? Oh God, where are you now?

We, as a nation, have had way too much practice at asking these questions given the astoundingly heartbreaking events that have unfolded in recent years for many of our fellow citizens. These acts of seemingly random violence have a chilling effect on our mindsets and outlooks. We become afraid for ourselves, for our loved ones, for our way of life. It is hard to clearly hear the word of God whispering in our ear when anxiety is thundering so much more loudly.

Given the bewildering array of fear, violence, and extremism we have experienced nationally and globally, these are times when we have to decide whether we will live as a People of Fear or as a People of Promise. People of Fear only know one thing: Stay safe. Buy a bigger lock and stronger chain. Invest in a more powerful personal weapon, learn how to shoot at things, and keep it handy in a glove compartment, purse, briefcase, pocket, or loaded under the pillow at night. Protect one's own rights and get rid of any dissent that might threaten the precarious balance that takes so much energy to preserve. It was probably People of Fear who arranged for Jesus to be crucified. It's not too difficult to be a People of Fear.

Not that being People of Promise is any easier. It is not. It is probably harder, but when it seems as though the mooring has been lost, People of Promise grope around in the abyss to find the anchor again. They look for the Light because they know it is there somewhere in the dark. People of Promise stand firm upon the rock of faith because to stand anywhere else is a slippery slope.

So where do we turn as our faith collides with our fear? What sweet spot is out there to provide comfort and reassurance that everything will be okay? When the hand of God seems so far off, what image can we hold near to remember that we are the beloved of God now and always?

Over the centuries, many have turned to the ancient and beautiful Psalm 23 for comfort. "The LORD is my Shepherd . . ." is so familiar and used in so many settings we can sink into its comforting embrace with merely those first five words.

I would love to know the life story of the person who wrote Psalm 23. It is credited to King David, but we don't really know who wrote it. Yet someone in that ancient desert land so long, long ago had a story to tell of God's grace in his life; someone who longed for God with a terrible thirst. Who walked in valleys of deep darkness and found God there. Who stopped running long enough to realize that goodness and mercy are what God joyfully offered when he let God catch up with him. The author heard the voice of God calling and he recognized it. He recognized it and then he wrote about it. He is telling us his story. It is an ancient story because ours is a God who has brooded over the world for millennia, faithfully watching like a shepherd. Calling to us. Waiting until we recognize his voice. Calling with a consistent passion for us that drowns out the harsh sounds of live bullets in a movie theater.

The term "Hebrew Scripture" is the compilation of the Jewish writings that form part of our biblical canon. It is a contemporary way of distinguishing that which Christians call "The Old Testament."

This ancient and well-known song is part of the Hebrew Scripture and would have been something Jesus studied as a young man. It is a distillation of hundreds of years of struggle and learning the ways of this "God" who had called the people of Israel into being as God's people. The very word "Israel" means "those who have struggled with God."[16]

What did it take for the people of Israel to learn that Yahweh was like a shepherd? In so many other places in Hebrew Scripture, Yahweh sounds like a vengeful and angry divine being. This side of the divine nature, however, presents something different. If they rushed off in pursuit of some golden idol, they would eventually be brought back into the fold. When choices they made as a people led to catastrophe and exile, God went with them. When they got scared and lost their way, Yahweh went in search of them to find them and restore them. Through prophets and sages Yahweh spoke to them. Through historical events, God was present to them and, like the family trees from which each of us spring, Yahweh and the Hebrew people built their history together eon after eon. Psalm 23 is a composite of

The evolution of the name for "God" is a study unto itself. To the early Hebrews, the name of God was so sacred it was not to be spoken. One word they used was YHWH or "Yahweh" as a way to talk about this deity they worshipped. It is used here in this chapter to suggest the ancient relationship between God and the people.

---

16 Craig Barnes, "Sheep on the Run (Psalm 23)," *The Christian Century*, February 13–20, 2002, 17. Copyright by The Christian Century Foundation and prepared for Religion Online by Ted and Winnie Brock.

someone's personal experience with a God who just doesn't quit. It is a love song about how God cares for us.

The image of green pastures and still waters that "revive the soul" actually exists here in the Green Mountain State of Vermont, especially during the summer. Throughout the entire year we are refreshed with God's love song. In the spring, we live in a land lush with new life. Water rushes with abandon, waking the wild grasses from their winter sleep; the earth is wet and spongy from the melting winter snows and spring rains; sunny days quickly coax the grass and plants to green up and flower. Summer looms and with it our memories and anticipation of green pastures, deep pools of favorite swimming holes, and gorgeous sunsets along Lake Champlain framed against the Adirondack Mountains in the distance. But this was not so in the land where this song was written.

Youth from Jerusalem and Palestine who participate in the annual Kids4Peace program come to Vermont with an interesting question: "Are the mountains really green?" They live in the same ancient and ancestral land where Psalm 23 was composed and where the mountains are brown and the land is filled with rocks, dirt, sand, and dust. Life was hard and tenuous back in the ancient time when Psalm 23 was written. Sheep were grazed where crops could not grow because fertile soil that could grow food was not wasted on feeding animals. Water was always at a premium. Danger in the forms of wolves or mountain lions could lurk behind any boulder. The only safety for any sheep grazing was the shepherd who kept watch. Even then the shepherd might only have a slingshot or spear and his courage to defend himself and his flock from a hungry pack of predators. Green pastures and plentiful water were not part of the regular landscape and would be a secret oasis known only to the shepherd who would guide his flock, coaxing and luring them to "come this way. I know the way. Come with me. I know a place that will deeply refresh you."

It is the nature of God to know what we need when we are in the midst of our daily lives and, if we listen, to lead us to a place where

Kids4Peace (www.k4p.org) is a grassroots interfaith youth movement dedicated to ending conflict and inspiring hope in Jerusalem and other divided societies around the world. Their mission is to build interfaith communities that embody a culture of peace and empower a movement for change.

we can just be tended by this gentle hand that knows what we need and provides that abundantly. We don't just get a drink of water. We get deep spiritual lagoons to refresh our longing and thirst for God, for meaning, for community, and companionship along the way.

But we can't rest in that idyllic place forever because God did not create us to be kept safely sheltered in a box. We are created for life and to live in a state of journey. We are created to be a People of Promise, not a People of Fear. At some point, we must move on to different spiritual terrain. There are wide plains that stretch with options and amazing choices from horizon to horizon. There are forks in the road forcing us to choose a direction, not knowing where it might lead. There are rivers and chasms to cross, bridges to build, and obstacles to overcome. Mountaintop experiences await along with deep, dark valleys where the light of day cannot penetrate and our shadow sides of fear come out of hiding, drawn forth by illness, loss of job, financial insecurity, death of a loved one, betrayal, starting life over, the ending of a relationship, or terror vicariously experienced on the nightly news. The wrenching and ancient cry, "Oh God, where are you now?" echoes against the silent walls of our fears.

Each of us has a default mode when we walk through the valley of the shadow of death. Each of us has a spontaneous response when we get scared. The default setting for sheep is to run. Bolting helter-skelter, not knowing where to go, just trying to escape, and in that running, they get lost, and sometimes follow the leader off the cliff. Where do you automatically turn and what do you instinctively do without thinking when you get scared? The late psychologist Rollo May once wrote: "It is an ironic habit of human beings to run faster when we have lost our way."[17] There's probably a little sheep in all of us from time to time, wandering off, quickly spooked, running away, easily lost, feeling defenseless against the pursuing wolves that harass us, imagined or real.

Psalm 23 is the reminder that our way out of the valley of despair is to trust in a God who will not lead us off a cliff but rather back to where we belong. A table of abundance is set for us in the midst of all that assaults us—even in the midst of our enemies—and we are invited to eat joyously and generously at a table lavishly filled with God's constancy, love, and grace.

And "goodness and mercy shall follow me all the days of my life."

---

17 Rollo May, AZQuotes.com, Wind and Fly LTD, 2016. http://www.azquotes.com/author/9646-Rollo_May, accessed October 28, 2016.

The ancient word used for "follow" is also the word for "persecute" and "pursue." How does it change things to think about goodness and mercy as being something that pursues you? Not pursuit such as little happy puppies might do while romping at your heels, but active qualities of God that are tracking you down. Goodness will keep pursuing you and mercy will keep chasing you until it feels as though they are persecuting you with their relentless presence. Goodness and mercy. That is a pretty powerful image of a loving God who never quits even in the face of tragedies that stun our sensibilities. That is the icon of a guide who knows the way and leads us toward the spiritual waters that fill our longing; a beckoning light in the valley of shadows; a "hound of heaven" pursuing with goodness and mercy.

God's ancient story is part of the DNA of our own personal stories and is not limited to a long ago time in a desert land. The ancient writer had a life story with God that led him to write Psalm 23. He describes an active and vibrant presence that is very much alive and well, available to us and out ahead of us beckoning: "Come. I know the way. Follow me and I'll take you there."

"Hound of Heaven" is a poem written by Francis Thompson (1859–1907). It describes the attempt to flee from God, only to discover that God has always been present, offering kindness and compassion if one stops running away long enough to realize it. The poem itself can be found here: www.bartleby.com/236/239.html.

Remembering that ancient story is part of what Psalm 23 is designed to do. When "enemies" assault you, remember God's ancient story. When your default mode kicks into high gear with fear or running away, remember God's ancient story. When you thirst and hunger for spiritual food, for righteousness, for justice, remember God's ancient story.

The LORD is *your* shepherd, good People of God. You shall not be left wanting. He makes you to lie down in green pastures and leads you beside still waters. He revives your soul and guides you along right pathways for his name's sake.

Though you walk through the valley of things that feel like the shadow of death, fear nothing evil, for God is with you. His rod and staff are there to comfort you and keep you near. God spreads a table before you and he does this in the presence of those who trouble you. He anoints your head with oil, in the manner of kings. Your cup runs over because it is lavishly filled with good things and abundant generosity.

And goodness and mercy? Well, goodness and mercy will hound you all the days of your life, and you will dwell in God's way forever.

Connecting with People of Promise

There is power in using Psalm 23 in a pastoral way, especially when you change the first person pronouns (my, I, me, and mine) to second person pronouns (you and your) and add someone's name.

You might try this activity in one of two ways: 1) a closing prayer with an individual with whom you might be sharing a pastoral visit; or 2) as a group closing activity. In this second option, a leader starts and reads the part of "Reader One" to the person on their left, using that person's first name where *"N"* appears in the script. This person becomes "Reader Two" and says the lines for Reader Two to the person on their left, who becomes "Reader Three," and so on. Keep going even if you read more than once so that everyone gets a chance to experience this. For example:

Reader One: The LORD is your shepherd, *N.* Do not be afraid.

Reader Two: He makes you to lie down in green pastures, *N.*

Reader Three: And leads you beside the still waters.

Reader Four: He revives your soul, *N* . . .

Reader Five: . . . and guides you along right pathways for his name's sake.

Reader Six: Though you walk through the valley of things that feel like the shadow of death . . .

Reader Seven: . . . fear nothing evil, *N,* for God is with you.

Reader Eight: His rod and staff are there to comfort you and keep you near.

Reader Nine: God spreads a table before you, *N,* and he does this in the presence of those who trouble you.

Reader Ten: He anoints your head with oil, in the manner of kings and queens.

Reader Eleven: Your cup runs over, *N,* because it is lavishly filled with good things and abundant generosity.

Reader Twelve: Goodness and mercy will hound you all the days of your life, *N* . . .

All Readers: . . . and you will dwell in God's way forever. Amen.

Note: Consider enhancing the experience with ambiance such as a quiet setting where the group will not be interrupted, soft lighting, candles, meditational music, and/or incense. This exercise works best in a small group.

Pondering

Reflect on the impact of the above exercise. How does this change your personal experience of Psalm 23? What connections do you make to God? To each other? What is God speaking to you?

PART THREE

The Bleeding Edge

For God alone my soul in silence waits;
    from him comes my salvation.
He alone is my rock and my salvation,
    my stronghold, so that I shall not be greatly shaken.
                        (Ps. 62:1–2, BCP)

The Bleeding Edge

One fascinating phenomenon of nature is that of crystal formation. They are lovely, solidified collections of minerals formed when certain types of liquids evaporate, leaving shape, color, and a solid surface in its place that can reflect light (or not). Crystals can be as hard as diamonds or as fragile as a snowflake, and under the right circumstances they continue to grow. The best crystals are the ones that grow slowly. But what always intrigues me is that when crystals grow, they grow on their outer edge, giving new meaning to the phrase "the growing edge."

One's personal growing edge is like that of a crystal—slow growth, gathering up of new material to incorporate into the structure, beauty and mystery formed over time. But while not all crystals are sharp as a blade, some are and they can cut like a knife. Life circumstances as well—those experiences we gather up as we go along—sometimes have a bleeding edge to them for they can, and do, cut like a knife.

It is in those places, when our heart is broken by life's situations and we do not really know what will happen next, that God shows up with new information totally outside our expectations and well-laid plans.

Perhaps some of the most powerful scriptural stories of life's bleeding edge are found in the events surrounding Holy Week. The next three stories wander through some of the events surrounding this annual time in the church's liturgical calendar: Mary Magdalene's overwhelming grief that turns to joy; Judas's betrayal and his eventual life choice; and the disciples' traveling on the road to Emmaus. This section concludes with a personal memoir outlining my own bleeding edge and what occurred after many years of "being finished" with God, church, and clergy.

Each of these stories embraces experiences that might have seemed overwhelming and devastatingly final at the time. It is God's good time and persistent faithfulness, however, that turn a painful bleeding edge into an experience of resurrection. It may take more than three days in the tomb to find us, but find us he will, for there is always a resurrection. Always.

Holy Week is the time in the Christian calendar year that begins on Palm Sunday and concludes on Easter morning. It outlines the stories of Jesus's last week on earth, his death, and resurrection.

CHAPTER 8

Whom Do You Seek?

A Story of Mary Magdalene at the Tomb

Reflect: What resurrection story have you witnessed in your own life?

Read: John 20:1–18

SCRIPTURE SAYS IT was still dark when she gathered up her things and walked in the silent coolness of the very early morning to return to the place where her world had collapsed. Mary Magdalene probably didn't pay attention to the gravel that crunched under her feet in the quiet dawn as she trudged back up the road where, just two days earlier, a noisy, bustling mix of thrill-seekers and mourners had followed the garish parade of soldiers and prisoners up the hill called Golgotha where the Romans put people to death in the most barbaric way they could think of: crucifixion. It was meant to be a deterrent to other people who would defy Roman authority; even though Jesus had been condemned as an insurrectionist by dubious means, there still was no stopping a political machine once it got rolling. It all felt so different now. Where were all the crowds? Had everyone gone back to the regularity of their everyday lives? Did they not even recognize that other lives had been cruelly and devastatingly changed forever? It was quiet now, however, and a good time to be about the business to which she wanted to attend.

It had been a hard few days. Jesus's arrest and crucifixion took all of them by surprise and there was no answer to the ancient question: "Why do such bad things happen to such good people?" To say it was a disaster would be to underestimate the impact on their lives. Their lives had been ripped wide open.

Luckily, someone with some kind of authority had been able to get hold of Jesus's body and lay it in a nearby tomb so that dogs and carrion birds wouldn't desecrate it any more than it already had been. On the day he died, there hadn't been time for the women to do what they normally did in those circumstances: wash the body gently, anoint it lovingly with fragrant oils and bittersweet tears, then wrap it carefully in bands of cloth, all the while lifting up the memories of the loved one and whispering to the soul that had departed. Mary couldn't go the next day since it was the Sabbath and no work was to be done on that holy day. She had to wait and wait and wait. And in her waiting, she had to wrestle with her own grief in her own ways.

It must have seemed like a scene from a first-century science-fiction movie when she got there and found that the massive stone that had blocked the entrance had been rolled away and his body was gone. Who had gotten here first? Who had disturbed the tomb? He was gone! Had the authorities come back and not even let him rest in death? Hadn't they done enough already? Who was hounding him even yet?

At that point, all the protective "Mother Tiger" instincts kicked in and she ran back to get the others. Not fearing for her safety, only intent on getting help to find him. She roused Peter and John, the beloved disciple, but even after they came to see for themselves, they didn't know to do anything different than go home with their grief and confusion renewed. It was all just too much to bear. "Mother Tiger Mary" was left alone, plaintively weeping the words over and over: "Where have you gone?" and feeling the most abandoned that she had ever been in her entire life.

Through the blur of her tears, she became aware of the presence of another standing nearby; she assumed it was the gardener asking her why she was weeping and whom was she seeking. "Please, sir. They have taken away my LORD and I do not know where they have laid him. If you have carried him away, tell me where you have laid him and I will take him away." How odd that the "gardener" knew her name: "Mary." It was confusing and disconcerting because that sounded exactly like the way Jesus would call her name with an intimacy that gazed right through her: "Mary."

In the stunned silence, many of the things Jesus had said that hadn't always made a lot of sense at the time became stunningly clear. A veil was lifted from her eyes, mind, and heart and she knew. It was unbelievable, but there he was in front of her. The magnitude of what he kept trying to get them to understand was all too evident and she finally recognized that she had been walking with the presence of a living God who had been doing something new all along.

She would never find his body in the tomb. He wasn't there. He had risen, as strange as that sounded. In an instant, mourning turned to miracle, and if it was hard for her to believe, it was going to be even harder to explain to the disciples. But there was the evidence, still, of the empty tomb and the risen LORD in front of her. The empty tomb was something concrete. That one wouldn't be explained away so easily.

Here we are thousands of years later still wondering about the same tale on Easter morning. Still pondering: "Is this really true? How can that be?" We are fortunate. We have various versions of the Easter story neatly spread out for us in our liturgical readings during the events of Holy Week and Easter Week: Palm Sunday; Judas's betrayal; the Last Supper; Jesus's arrest, torture, crucifixion, and resurrection; Jesus showing up in the midst of disciples who were hiding in an upper room, and to other disciples who were escaping town on the road to Emmaus. We can visit the story whenever we choose and take it in palatable bits and pieces to chew on at our leisure. The real event, however, cascaded and crashed around the disciples in a very short period of time. They didn't have the luxury of putting it down to go do something else when the situation got too intense.

It was a living nightmare, one that threatened to undo all that Jesus had done in his lifetime. One moment they were part of a solid group with direction and mission, fellowship, and purpose. The next minute they were cast adrift against their will or ability to control events. The road they traveled took a turn that was not of their choosing, much like the unexpected and unwelcome life events that test our own resolve, resilience, integrity, and courage from time to time.

In looking at the Easter story, there is a narrative that is not written down. We might just find a spiritual journey that is not that dissimilar from our own. Stories in Scripture can become so familiar; we just breeze on by without really thinking because we know how the story will go and how it all turns out. Year after year it turns out the same. It is crucial to remember, however, that the people in any of the Scripture stories didn't know how their story would turn out. They had to walk the same path of struggle, doubt, and faith that we all walk in our daily lives. What we learn from how God moved in their lives shines a light on how God might well be moving in our lives as well.

Consider the story of Peter, who is bound up in the Holy Week story. Peter was justifiably wracked with guilt and his own failure to be the perfect disciple he imagined himself to be. Here he was— one of the inner circle—who had sworn to Jesus in front of the other disciples that he would never betray Jesus. He would die with him first. He, Peter, was so strong, so loyal, so trustworthy. So human. He got scared and he did the one thing he thought he would never do: he ran away. He ran. Abandoned Jesus to the authorities and then pretended that he didn't even know the man. It was the failure of a lifetime that would haunt him for the rest of his days, but it was also a denial of everything Peter thought he, himself, was. Now that's a dark place.

So what happened? What happened to Peter? What transformed him from that dark night of the soul to become the confident, articulate, courageous, daring apostle and leader of the early church who threw caution to the wind and began healing the sick, baptizing new believers, and speaking out in defiance to the authorities when he was arrested and warned to stop doing what he was doing?

Something of an amazing magnitude transformed him, revolutionized him beyond a shadow of a doubt into a new person of courage: forgiven, restored, and made more than whole again. Transformed into someone God knew he could be all along. What *was* that precipitating event that changed his life forever so suddenly?

What was it that happened to all the disciples and followers of Jesus, men and women, that galvanized them from the ragtag, leaderless crew that they were after the crucifixion to become one of the most powerful forces for love, healing, and forgiveness that the world had ever seen? They rocketed from a personal jumble of grief, disillusionment, and despair to become transfixed in amazement, astonishment, and disbelief as Jesus appeared first here and then there—at the tomb, then on the road to Emmaus, then in the upper room where they were hiding—all in the course of one week.

The only window we have to help us understand the story of what happened in the resurrection is to look at what happened in the lives of the women and men who knew Jesus and who were there. Something pretty amazing happened because of what we see in how their lives were transformed. There was no other force powerful enough to cause that kind of change in each of their lives. Jesus still lived among them: not figuratively, not in memory, nor as an inspiration. Jesus was living among them still. Death had no dominion. Really.

And it is here, at the gaping, scary darkness of the empty tomb, that the Gospel writer invites us to ponder the question Jesus asked Mary: "Whom do *you* seek?"

What resurrection story are you a witness to? Or are you in the middle of your own Good Friday or in the limbo-land of Holy Saturday? We can't know the power of God's light until we have lived in the tyranny of the darkness. So, "Whom do you seek?"

God is not here in death. Jesus is not in the tomb where you might expect to find him. He has risen. He is moving ahead and inviting us to join him. Why? Because God has not given up on us. God has something in mind for this sometimes crazy-quilt world we live in. Jesus comes personally with the assurance that there is nothing, truly nothing, that God cannot turn around into something good and holy, as hard as that might be to believe sometimes.

Sometimes our personal Good Fridays last a long time. Sometimes we rest on a never-ending borderline of Holy Saturday. Sometimes God's resurrection takes more than three days to find us, but find us it will, for there is always a resurrection. Always.

We are an Easter People. We live on the resurrection side of the cross and like the disciples who cowered in a nightmare one minute and burst out of their own tomb of fear the next, we have our own story to tell. We live in a world hungry to hear that kind of good news.

Like the first people to see the empty tomb, we are witnesses to God's greatness and dominion over everything, even death.

Easter is not a day or a season. It is a way of living with the assurance that God is deeply, unconditionally in love with us. God discards all the obstacles we place in the way and replaces them with abundance and absolute devotion that is showered upon us willingly, joyfully, and freely. In the sealed tombs of our own lives and our own making, God comes calling again and again to roll away the stone; to lighten our darkness, heal our wounds, and bind up our broken hearts in the way that only God can. That's the miracle. That's the Good News.

"But can you prove it?" one might ask.

No, I probably can't prove it to anyone's satisfaction who might be asking that question. Then again, neither could Mary as she ran to tell the other disciples Jesus's amazing message that he was back. I'm not sure they believed her at first either. But something extraordinary happened that turned their lives around from grieving, broken, disappointed disciples to energetic apostles of joy, hope, vigor, and influence who literally changed the world.

Perhaps it is right there in that question of proof where the fire of faith is best kindled, however. Faith is as elusive, yet as perceptible as the wind. Can anyone prove there is wind? One can define scientifically why the wind materializes, but is it not best "proven" by what we observe the wind doing? We cannot bottle it up in a jar, but we can see where it has been and where it is going as it crosses a field of wheat. We cannot touch and hold it in our hands, but we welcome its whisper caressing our cheeks on a hot day. We cannot control its power, but we try to live in harmony with it. It is what I see around me that "proves" to me there is such a thing as wind. So even if you say you have no faith, you already have experience with believing something that you cannot see. We take it on faith that the wind exists because we see and experience its impact.

Just so, it is what we see in the lives of other people that demonstrate the hand of God at work quietly, subtly, and magnificently. It is in stories such as the one we are considering here that tease me to ponder the mystery of the radical change that overtook the disciples. It is the puzzling presence of God's hand in my own story that suggests coincidences are God's way of staying anonymous. It is the forces for good operating in our world, regardless of church affiliation or not, that convince me God doesn't care who gets the credit. It is love on the loose that matters.

This story in Scripture ends, but it was not the end of God's story. It was the new beginning of the next chapter of God. God is there in what you might think is unanswered prayer. God is there in the tiniest distant pinprick of light and hope shining in the darkness. God is there in inscrutable mystery as well as in everyday incidents.

So, "Whom do *you* seek?"

Connecting with Mary Magdalene

Welcome to Mary's world. You have found the love of your life—someone who makes you feel whole and complete, loved and cherished. It is as though the day is only half bright, only half alive, only half appealing if you are not together. Suddenly, however, everything came crashing down when he was arrested so unfairly, taken away, and slaughtered mercilessly. To learn that the betrayal was brought about by one of the trusted disciples completes the terrible treachery. It is your broken heart and your broken life that stagger to the tomb on that early morning after the Sabbath. In spite of the huge boulder blocking the entrance to his tomb, you could still be as close to him as you can get. You'll take it because it is all there is. What happens next is not even on your radar because you are too focused on your loss. Quietly, at the edge of the garden, someone appears. You are not sure at first. It can't be—can it? Looking closer as the morning light shifts, you realize it is he. "He is back? It can't be? How did he do that? He was just dead!" What do you feel? What do you think? What do you want? What has it been like to live through the events of the past week, from the triumphal entry straight through to Jesus's death and now his being alive again?

Pondering

Sometimes our personal Good Fridays last a long time. Sometimes God's resurrection takes more than three days to find us, but find us it will. What has been your personal experience with your own Good Friday and Resurrection moments?

CHAPTER 9

Good News Comes— Even for the Betrayer

A Story of Judas Iscariot

Reflect: When have you been betrayed?
Read: Matthew 26:14–16, 47–50

Holy Week is probably one of the most challenging and difficult weeks in the Christian calendar. It begins with the parades of Palm Sunday, when the streets are crowded with hope-filled people waving palms and branches. The air is filled with shouts of "Hosanna! Blessed is the one who comes in the name of the Lord!" (Mark 11:9). It is tempting to jump straight from that over to Easter morning, when all the awful stuff that occurs in between is over and we are greeted with a sunrise bright with hope, amazed disciples, tears of joy and wonder at a miracle of miracles that no one could really wrap their heads around very quickly.

The entire backdrop of Holy Week is one that describes some of the unfortunate things that people sometimes do to other people all through the history of humankind: treachery and betrayal, a kangaroo court, denial, disbelief, broken hearts, ruined lives. It touches on fragments that are not a norm in our culture: torture leading to death by suffocation, a rushed burial in someone's borrowed tomb, a promising life tragically cut short, and scattered disciples struggling to answer the question, "What just happened?"

The catalyst for the intensity of this week revolves around the actions of one man: Judas Iscariot. We don't often hear about Judas. We probably don't even want to think about him, except during Holy Week when he becomes the trigger for tragedy. His name has become synonymous with evil betrayal. The phrase "You Judas!" does not take much explanation in our common idioms. While the Gospels and Judas's role in everything was written long after the events that he was involved with, he wasn't always seen as a person who was a traitor.

Biblical scholar Bishop N. T. Wright suggests:

> We constantly have to remind ourselves, in reading this story, that when Jesus said "one of you will betray me," the other eleven disciples didn't at once turn around and point knowingly at Judas. . . . As far as the other eleven were concerned, he was one of them, sharing their common life, a trusted and valued friend and comrade. He had seen Jesus' wonderful healings. He had heard the parables. He had agreed with Peter that Jesus was the Messiah. He had come with them into Jerusalem, singing Hosannas, laying his coat on the road, watching in glee as Jesus upset tables, chairs, coins and doves in the Temple. He wasn't any different from the rest of them.[18]

He was one of the twelve who were trusted, who had followed through thick and thin, and in whom Jesus saw promise. Jesus spent days and, according to some scriptural accounts, a lot of patience, hoping that all of them would begin to see what he, Jesus, was trying to teach them. All so they might truly hold the keys to the kingdom of God's love, justice, compassion, mercy, and forgiveness. Even though there was grumbling among the disciples from time to time and jockeying for position as to whom was the most important, no one expected one of their own to sell out Jesus to the authorities for a handful of silver coins.

So why did Judas do what he did? What would have motivated this follower who held a position of authority in the group of disciples? He was the treasurer. He managed the money that kept them going and distributed funds to the poor, following Jesus's admonition. What were the hopes and ambitions that Judas brought along with him into

---

18 N. T. Wright, *Matthew for Everyone, Part Two: Chapters 16–28* (Louisville, KY: Westminster John Knox Press, 2004), 151.

his discipleship that apparently were not fulfilled? What was his motivation that caused him to break ranks with the others? There are various theories about this question.

Some scholars have suggested that Judas might have been associated with a group known as the Zealots or even a group called the "sicarii." [19] This latter group consisted of professional assassins committed to extreme nationalism who were working to drive the Romans from Palestine and restore Israel to its former greatness. Could it be that Jesus's popularity fueled Judas's own fervent hopes for a popular uprising right there in Jerusalem during the days of Passover? There were thousands of pilgrims gathered for these high, holy days of the Jewish faith. It would have been perfect timing politically to elevate Jesus to the stature of king, and Judas would be there right beside him, managing the keys to the deposit box.

Yet Jesus kept insisting he was not that kind of king. Everything he did was aimed at some different kind of kingdom. Could it be that Judas was severely disappointed that the pomp and popularity generated during their arrival on what we call Palm Sunday was not seized in the moment? Might Judas have been hoping to exploit that time for what he thought was a greater good? The person perpetrating that action might not always see that which we call betrayal as betrayal.

There are some who suggest that Judas had become disillusioned with Jesus's seemingly weak use of that kind of power. Did Judas see an opportunity to manipulate Jesus into an untenable position, thereby forcing his hand in a direction Judas felt was important? Was he hopeful he would see Jesus's fireworks at work, breaking free from his captors in a potent display of command? Did Judas, himself, feel betrayed by Jesus? Maybe he never intended for Jesus to die. Who knows? Ultimately, the answer to the question "Why?" doesn't matter.

> However we look at it, the tragedy of Judas is that he refused to accept Jesus as he was and tried to make him what he wanted him to be. It is not Jesus who can be changed by us, but we who must be changed by Jesus. We can never use him for our purposes; we must submit to be used for his. The tragedy of Judas is that of a man who thought he knew better than God.[20]

---

19 William Barclay, *The New Daily Study Bible: The Gospel of Matthew, Vol. 2* (Louisville, KY: Westminster John Knox Press, 2001), 388.
20 Ibid.

The reality is that Judas wasn't the only one who betrayed Jesus. Every one of the disciples ran away. That betrayal must have been heartbreaking for Jesus in his hour of deepest need, and yet he still loved them. In each of the disciples there were such human flaws, but Jesus always saw their blessings and sought to draw them out by bringing the disciples gifts and skills into God's work in the world. Even the passion and impulsivity of Peter was channeled into keen and strong leadership. Jesus honored the love and devotion of Mary, the sister of Lazarus, who spent the equivalent of a year's salary to simply anoint Jesus's feet with costly perfume as a generous gesture. The intensity and quickly provoked reactions of James and John (the disciples Jesus called "Sons of Thunder") were tempered so they might transform their impetuosity into servanthood in spite of the unexpected storms of life. Perhaps Jesus saw the goodness in Judas that we have a tough time seeing.

Can a person like Judas ever receive redemption? Does God's forgiveness extend even to the person whose choice led to the murder of God's Son? Judas clearly felt remorse for his action. He tried to return the money to the High Priests and confessed that he had betrayed an innocent man whose blood was now on his hands. But the priests had gotten what they wanted and were done with Judas. It was his problem now.

In spite of his faithless action in the Garden of Gethsemane, Jesus still greeted Judas with the beloved endearment of "friend." Judas's despair became so great, he could only think of one thing to do in order to end his pain: suicide. In the midst of all he had heard Jesus teach about forgiveness and God's love, he missed the point that God's love, compassion, and mercy were there for him as well. Perhaps he got so caught up in the "tasks" of being a disciple, he forgot to keep his eyes on God.

When betrayed, we sometimes struggle to forgive the one who has deeply hurt us. Sometimes we are the betrayer thinking we know greater than God. Sometimes we try to make Jesus into our likeness rather than following where he leads, especially when it is where we would rather not go. Sometimes we forget to keep our eyes on God. Sometimes, like Judas, we are desperate to know we are already forgiven but are not willing or able to see that possibility. I wonder how the story would have turned out if Judas had realized he was already forgiven.

The story of Holy Week is one story that does not end in the devastation of betrayal and the finality of death, however. The story moves on to that hope-filled morning of Easter—but only after going through the darkness of Good Friday. Easter and Good Friday are linked together. You cannot have one without the other. The betrayal by Judas that leads to the darkness of Good Friday is meaningless without the redemption that shows up on Easter morning. God's love shouts to the world that God is bigger than death. Forgiveness, mercy, and love trump even the worst betrayal.

Even for Judas.

Connecting with Judas

How did it all change so quickly? This wasn't the plan. I didn't think it was going to go like this. How badly have I messed things up? I have to let Jesus know I didn't mean for it to turn out this way. He has to know I had good intentions. I love him. I know he loves me. He'll understand. He really loves me, and he looked so resigned when they arrested him and led him away. Let me try to fix this. Oh, God, I am so sorry. Please . . . I would give my life if I could fix this—if I could save him.

What is the goodness that Jesus saw in Judas?

Pondering

Good Friday and Easter morning are intimately linked. You cannot have one without the other. Good Friday without Easter is a meaningless tragedy. Easter without Good Friday is jellybeans and bunnies. How do you hold these two things together? Are they a paradox? Where is God in that for you? Have you ever gotten so caught up in the "tasks" of church life that you forgot to keep your eyes on God?

CHAPTER 10

The Breaking of the Bread

A Story of the Disciples on the Road to Emmaus

Reflect: Where have you discovered Jesus?

Read: Luke 24:13–35

THIS STORY IN the Gospel of Luke occurs on the same day the disciples discovered Jesus was no longer in the tomb. That day we call Easter precipitated a number of appearances by Jesus that are reported in various scriptural accounts. While we can unpack these resurrection stories week by week and fit them into our worship timetable, these initially reported appearances by Jesus happened very close together in a relatively short period of time.

This story in the Gospel of Luke finds us zeroing in on two disciples: Cleopas and one who is not identified. Apparently they have decided to go home now that Jesus is dead. Somehow they have managed to get out of Jerusalem undetected and are traveling toward the town of Emmaus while on their way to somewhere else. They had been in Jerusalem when Mary came running to tell the disciples that Jesus was still alive. However, even Mary's eyewitness of angelic visitation and the mystery of the empty tomb were not enough to overcome their own inclination to give up and just go home where life might be a lot safer and a whole lot simpler.

Their hopes that Jesus was the one who would redeem Israel were crushed. Their expectations and ambitions had been nailed to a cross where their hopes died. His miracles were now merely a fading memory and his compelling personality was a whisper in the wind. Their disorientation and loss were bewildering. Perhaps they had not yet reached the stage of grief where they would wrap their heads and hearts around their own sense of betrayal of Jesus having "left them." Things would just never be the same.

During the long walk on the dusty road, a stranger catches up with them and, as travelers do when meeting up with each other, they swap stories. Only it seems very odd that this stranger coming from the direction of Jerusalem seems to be the only person totally clueless about what has taken place in the city just a few days before. So, Cleopas and his traveling partner enlighten this stranger about Jesus, "who was a prophet mighty in deed and word before God and all the people" (Luke 24:19), and how their hopes had ended so savagely with Jesus's death.

Oddly, this stranger does not offer sympathy or words of comfort. Instead, he challenges their understanding and opens Scripture to them. He traces the story of God through Moses and the prophets, interpreting it in such a way that they become more enlightened about the slow and steady hand of God bringing salvation to the world. The sorrowing hearts of these escaping disciples are strangely stirred and encouraged.

It was only at dinner that night in some roadside inn that they realized who he was. It was not his physical appearance of height, weight, bearing, hair, or eye color that made them recognize him. It was what he did. It was his action in the breaking of the bread that offered the elegant and simple demonstration they needed for them to "get it."

They recognized Christ present with them not in words or a magic show, but in the simple act of reminding them what he had told them. He would be with them when they broke bread together. And then they knew it was true. Jesus was still with them, just as he said he would be. Once they recognized him, he no longer needed to be present physically for them to remember that indeed, their hopes for redemption were coming true, just not in the way they had thought.

To each other they said: "Were not our hearts burning within us while he was talking to us on the road, while he was opening the scriptures to us?" (Luke 24:32). It was Jesus all along, but their grief and disbelief blinded them to the world God was turning upside down with wonder and life. John Shea says:

> They remembered [Jesus] as a victim and passive recipient of cruel injustice visited upon him, rather than a willing participant in his own death. . . . When you remember Jesus as a reputation, a victim, a failure, and a dead man, him you will not see. . . . The key to finding the risen Christ is knowing where to look. [21]

A prayer in the Episcopal Church related to this story says: "O God, whose blessed Son made himself known to his disciples in the breaking of bread: Open the eyes of our faith that we may behold him in all his redeeming work."[22] Perhaps there is room in this Gospel story for us to be that unidentified disciple traveling with Cleopas on the road to Emmaus: yearning to have our hearts burn with the spiritual fire we know is out there somewhere, if only we could find it. What we might miss, however, is that "it"—God's spiritual hand at work—usually finds us.

> Episcopal priest, author, and consultant, the Rev. Sam Portaro, offers this thought: That we know of Easter at all is probably not because of those who were present. It's not because they went to Easter, but rather because Easter came to them. Easter came to Mary, who thought he was a gardener. Easter came to Thomas and others locked away in their fear. Easter came to companions on the road to Emmaus, and to disciples fishing by dawn's pale light. As important as the Easter event itself were those days that followed, days filled with Easter's patient, loving presence. They were days of companionship, and frequently included a meal. So it is that the community came to remember Jesus not upon the cross, but at table.[23]

---

21 John Shea, *The Spiritual Wisdom of the Gospels for Christian Preachers and Teachers: Matthew Year A, On Earth As It Is In Heaven* (Collegeville, MN: Liturgical Press, 2004), 169–70, 173.

22 "Collect for the Third Sunday of Easter," Book of Common Prayer (New York: Church Publishing, 1979), 224, hereafter noted as "BCP." A "collect" is a prayer designed to "collect" the thoughts and ideas of a particular theme in our worship.

23 Sam Portaro, "Missing Easter," April 8, 2012, http://credoveni.wordpress.com/2012/04/08/missing-easter/, accessed August 23, 2016.

While our Holy Meal, the Eucharist, draws from the Jewish Passover tradition in certain ways, it is different because our understanding is that our Eucharist is a sacred encounter with a Living God. God's promise is fulfilled in Jesus and we are liberated from death itself. Resurrection is our foundational spiritual story, for it is in our Holy Meal that we engage directly with making present the Living God who is still among us.

One word for that is the Greek word *anamnesis,* which sounds a lot like the word "amnesia," meaning when you no longer have a memory of something. But *anamnesis* means to "make present again." It means more than simply remembering Jesus or reenacting something Jesus did long ago. It means to make Jesus spiritually present with us again as we break bread together.

We don't just remember Jesus in the breaking of the bread. We make him present with us again. "This is my body, which is given for you. Do this in *anamnesis* of me. Do this for the *making present again* of me."[24] Jesus becomes known to us through the breaking of the bread; it is in our Holy Meal where we believe we directly engage with the Living God at our table.

The story of the road to Emmaus led those two disciples to find Jesus mystically in the breaking of the bread. Our own personal roads to find Jesus are not all that different. Hopes become dashed. Discouragement seems larger than life itself. We think things can never be the same again. But then, into the center of that foggy mist comes the image of two hands breaking bread in our presence just for us. Not for sustenance alone but for the inner assurance that, indeed, we are not alone because Jesus is there with us too.

One of our Eucharistic Prayers says it well: "Open our eyes to see your hand at work in the world about us. Deliver us from the presumption of coming to this Table for solace only, and not for strength; for pardon only, and not for renewal. Let the grace of this Holy Communion make us one body, one spirit in Christ, that we may worthily serve the world in his name." To which we respond: "Risen LORD, be known to us in the breaking of the Bread."[25]

Then we go back out into the world to tell our stories. Cleopas and his fellow traveler hurried back to Jerusalem to tell the other disciples of what had just transformed them from two weary and discouraged

---

24 St. Paul's Parish, Riverside, IL, http://stpaulsparish.org/education/documents/ Anamnesis_QA.pdf, accessed August 23, 2016.
25 BCP, 372.

people to trailblazers with new joy and hope in their hearts. It *wasn't* all over. Something new was beginning. It was time to be together again. Their life with Jesus was not over by a long shot. It was just beginning.

God will always get through the locked doors of our hearts. Always. Whether it is through the breaking of the bread or a kind word from an unexpected source. In a quiet "Aha!" moment or in the presence of a mystical oddity that we cannot explain away, God loves each of us so profoundly that we will not be left alone. Jesus travels the road to Emmaus with us even if we don't recognize him right away.

"Faith is not knowing where you are going, but going anyway."[26] God surely has faith in us because he travels life's roads with us in all times and through all things. We have only to stop and listen long enough to be found. As Meister Eckhart said in the fourteenth century, "God is [always] at home. It is we who have gone for a walk."[27]

Connecting with the Disciples on the Road to Emmaus

You are walking down the road heading out of Jerusalem along with your friend. The hope and promise you had believed in is dead. There is nothing left and no one left to carry you forward. Why stay exposed to the witch-hunt seeking out the other followers of Jesus? There is no place else to go except home, so you are on your way, grateful to be alive at least—still stunned by the swift-moving momentous events of the past week. The stranger who has joined you is an interesting mix of knowledge and naiveté. He can talk all day about Scripture but then doesn't even know about the horrible event that took place in the city of Jerusalem where he surely must have been staying.

What does it feel like to be walking on the road away from Jerusalem? A few days ago you were going in the opposite direction, excitedly heading toward that great city. What are the emotions going through your mind? What is it like to meet up with this stranger and tell him what just happened? What do you learn from him that you didn't know before? What goes through your mind as you sit at dinner together and he takes bread, blesses it, and breaks it in an amazing replication of the very same words and signs that Jesus used just a few short nights ago when you last gathered as a group? Where

---

26 The Rev. Kirk Alan Kubicek, "Second Sunday of Easter," sermon, April 23, 2006, http://archive.episcopalchurch.org/sermons_that_work_73147_ENG_HTM.htm.
27 "Weekly Seeds," May 4, 2014, www.ucc.org/feed-your-spirit/weekly-seeds/breaking-breadcompanions-on.html, accessed August 23, 2016.

did this stranger learn to do that? What do you wonder about? Why are you choosing to return to Jerusalem?

Pondering

What symbolic "road to Emmaus" have you been on in your life story? Have you possibly met up with God traveling the road with you but did not recognize him because he didn't appear as you expected? Was there an "Aha!" moment of recognition and acknowledgement? Did anything change for you from that experience?

CHAPTER 11

Who Will I Be When the Geese Fly North?

A Story of Carole

Reflect: Have you ever lost (or been found by) God?

Read: Psalm 139:1–13

THE BLEEDING EDGE of life plays out dramatically in the stories of Holy Week. The blazing fire of grief and disillusionment is not limited to Scripture alone, however. Many of us have such experiences in the course of our individual lives. Betrayal of trust, devotion gone awry, faithfulness and love misused and manipulated for dark purposes—these are part and parcel of the human condition. They cut like a knife, leaving a profound hurt that either heals over time or remains a gaping wound that becomes so familiar we no longer see it for what it is.

The last story explored in this chapter is a personal one. It is included because if ever I had the experience of resurrection surprise, it is here in my own story. Touching on the brokenness that comes when clergy do not recognize their power nor honor the dignity of their charges, this story also speaks of the healing of spirit and soul that only comes through time and God's grace. Like the disciples above, I, too, lost Jesus but discovered that Jesus never lost track of me.

Healing is somewhat like peeling an onion. There is always another layer to be found. Healing leaves a scar, but hopefully there comes a point when it no longer aches like it used to and feels more like a heartbreaking story that is yours to tell with authority, integrity, and dignity.

Such is this story. I discovered Psalm 139 when I began to reengage with life in a church after leaving twenty-three years earlier upon graduation from seminary. It so clearly outlined my sense of being tailed by the "hound of heaven." I discovered a grateful heart that after years of running away from God, God had not really run away from me, but persisted patiently until I was able to respond to God's call a second time.

The catalyst for such a dramatic ending to a promising call came in the form of a relationship, as abuse frequently does. Although the abuse I experienced was not physical, it was emotional blackmail and spiritual misuse of power and position. It generated from my years of participating in a youth program of religious drama at my home church that was extraordinary for what it attempted and achieved in that day and time. Over an eleven-year span of adolescent naiveté, teen idealism, and the enthusiasm of young adult energy, I was one of several who drew close to the assistant minister in our church and recognized God's call to ministry through his mentoring.

That call became polluted ever so imperceptibly as tendrils of exploitation and manipulation masked by teachings about God, love, commitment, and being unique wove their way around the hearts of those who fell captive to believing. Some became part of an "inner circle" in which the bond of sexuality became entwined with a commitment to God. In hindsight, the most poisonous thing was the way in which a relationship with and commitment to God got all tangled up in the relationship with and commitment to the clergyperson involved. There were elements of cult-like following that crept up on us slowly because it just all made sense at the time. It took many years of hard work to separate out the threads of abuse from the one thread of God's call.

In time I realized I could no longer run away from the painful past. It was my story and would always be so. I could either own it or continue to disown it, but it would still be my journey regardless. I had no intention of reengaging with any church or any life with God. I just wanted to make peace with myself. That was enough. The disillusionment of life within a church community continued to haunt me; church was no longer part of any plan I had for my family or myself.

And so it was on one bright and breezy day in September 1998 that I walked down the street in my hometown of Montpelier, Vermont, on an errand. I walked by the big stone church[28] in the middle of town as I had for many years, paying it no attention—but this day was different. The front door was wide open and the lights were all on inside. I could see the gold cross shining against the white background at the end of the aisle. I thought there must be a wedding taking place, but no one was around. No flowers or bride stuffed into a limo waiting for her grand procession to the altar. It also seemed odd there would be a wedding at eleven o'clock on a Tuesday morning. The most logical reason for the open doors to the church, therefore, must be that the carpet had been shampooed. Of course. With the sunny breeze, it was the perfect day to clean the carpets and let them dry. Mystery solved. Errand continued.

On my way back, however, my curiosity got the better of me and I timidly crept up the stone steps just to take a peek inside. Had anyone been present, I would have turned and bolted down the stairs. But I was alone. No one was there, even though the place was lit up as though something was expected to be happening at any time. I reached down to touch the carpet so that I would have a better idea of where to step on the damp carpet. It was dry. It was dry here and there and wherever I touched.

I was alone in a church for the first time in nearly twenty-three years when I didn't have to be there for a funeral or a wedding. The smell of the old wooden pews and the racks of books were familiar touchstones. The saints in the stained glass looked down upon me quietly as I walked down the aisle waiting for something to disturb the peaceful tranquility, hoping I could continue to be there on my own terms. The liturgical colors announced the season and my thoughts cast back to seminary days when that kind of thing mattered. I did not realize it at the time, but the "hound of heaven" had caught up with me at long last and was not about to let go easily.

That next Sunday, I attended worship for the first time in many years and I cried inconsolably all the way home. The burden I carried for so long of guilt, shame, failure, and betrayal, none of which were really my fault, were nothing compared to my grief at the way in which my innocence and the innocence of others had been manipulated by

---

28 Christ Episcopal Church in Montpelier, Vermont, was my first introduction to an
    Episcopal Church.

a clergyperson. It was a heartbreaking loss that I finally began to accept.

Autumn in Vermont is a poignant and nostalgic time when the dark of night can be wonderfully disrupted by the wild and desolate call of Canada geese notifying the world that they are leaving town for the winter. A few nights after my first visit to the church, I heard them fly overhead in the dark. I listened to them calling to each other in their nocturnal flight. They were invisible in the cloudy midnight sky, but I could hear them and wondered how they could possibly see where they were going as they flew on with such resolve and assurance. What mystery were they responding to as they flew the avian road maps that generations of migrations had stockpiled in their DNA? What covert power sustained their confidence? Why didn't they wait for the light of day when they could see where they were going?

But no, here they were flying at night, somehow knowing enough to follow whatever mystery it was that called them. They "heard it" in their bones and remembered to obey willingly and without question. It was what they were meant to do. In hindsight, maybe I should have done as much after running away from that same mystery for nearly a quarter of a century. While they were responding instinctively and obediently to a powerful summons that drew them to take flight, likewise, something equally insistent and mysterious had begun to make its presence known to me. I could feel it intuitively even if I could not be as instinctively obedient as the geese.

Had "it" been visible, I would surely have laid my hands on it in a death grip, for my inner world was roiling with pent-up energy, bitter loss, and unresolved pain. I had intentionally and purposefully locked up unresolved emotions, the grief of deep betrayal, and anything to do with religion or spirituality when I left "The Church" far behind. I had put God on a shelf like one might display a trophy award— ignored and left to collect dust.

On the outside, I'm sure I seemed much the same as every other day. However, on the inside, every molecule of my being knew that something long denied was yearning to crack open in surrender to a mystery that had spoken my name many years before. Although I had given it all up as a long-lost dream, a compelling drive was struggling to emerge and I had little control over its direction. My only choice was to hang on for the ride.

This annual rite of migration of geese is actually a measure of time: a trek south in the fall and a homecoming about six months later in the spring. As I lay listening to them in the dark night, I wondered who I would be when they flew north again. Something was changing and I knew I would not be the same person I was at that moment:

> I stand at a juncture and the path I'll follow is not
>   clear to me.
> Spirit calls my heart and I feel drawn into its
>   comfort.
> At night I hear the geese fly overhead, heading for
>   their winter feeding grounds.
> I'll miss them, for they are the harbinger of winter
>   and the herald of spring.
> And so, I wonder—who will *I* be—when the geese
>   fly north?[29]

Fast forward six months. Life had, indeed, moved on. I continued to worship; I had finally gotten brave enough to connect with the rector and told him my story. I timidly began to get involved in congregational life. I continued to follow that strange energy that would not let me go and began early steps toward discerning a call to the priesthood in the Episcopal Church. God had called me once. Twice now had I heard it and I was holding my heart out in response yet again.

The rector had invited me to preach at a small worship service on the Wednesday of Holy Week. Liturgically, this is when the story of Judas's betrayal is read. It was a fitting subject for my first sermon in many years. As I got dressed at home for the service, I was scared to death. Could I do it? Should I call in sick? I wanted to do this and would be disappointed if I didn't, but I was so terrified. What was I thinking when I agreed? Was I really called to the priesthood? What kind of craziness was that?

As this fear was beginning to take hold of me, I heard my husband calling me from outside. He told me to "come quickly." I dashed out into the driveway as he pointed up in the sky where there were flocks and flocks of Canada geese flying low overhead, making their way north. They were flying right over our house. We both remembered my question: "Who would I be when the geese flew north?" The coincidence was dumbfounding. Was this God's assurance that I was on the right track? I do not often experience the intrusion of God in such a fashion, but the timing was impeccable. I have since learned

---

29 The Rev. Carole Wageman, "Who Will I Be When the Geese Fly North?" (personal memoir, September 28, 1998).

that coincidences are not necessarily random things but perhaps more an experience of God staying anonymous.

After that, I continued moving warily with the discernment process in the Episcopal Church as I also reached deeper into my own healing. I was not sure I wanted the Church and I was not sure the Church would want me, but I was willing to consider what each next step brought. Slowly, over time, this discernment did eventually lead to my ordination as a priest in 2003. Today I continue to explore God's path before me at all times. I am grateful that God paid attention and never gave up hope in me; God managed to rekindle and restore courage and conviction, and heal a deeply wounded heart.

For Mary, Judas, the disciples on the road to Emmaus, and the many other lives touched by the Holy Week story, the loss of Jesus was initially a tragic blow. It became, however, the event through which God could work with astonishing, bewildering, and even shocking revelation of the existence of a mystical power so complete, so personal, so present that the only fitting words are: "I have *seen* the LORD!"

It must have been a difficult thing to grasp in the moment, however, when the familiar and recognizable seemed to be falling down around their feet. God working outside of the norm is not something we comprehend easily but perhaps that is our growing edge at work. God seems to stay anonymous a great deal of the time; yet, resurrection is persistent if we take a closer look at those things that haunt us. It just might not always look like we expect it to look.

Connecting with Wounded Healers

The story presented is a personal account. It is true. That which seemed like numerous coincidences at first I now consider to be God at work within me. Can you think of other people in Scripture or in real life who seemed to become aware of God's action in hindsight? What gets in the way of recognizing God at work outside the norm?

Pondering

Are there circumstances where you suspect God might be working within your own story? Is there anything that haunts you that feels unfinished? Can you consider that a resurrection moment might be lurking nearby?

Has God's anonymity ever presented itself to you in personal ways?

PART FOUR

Letting God Be God

The heavens declare the glory of God;
   and the firmament shows his handiwork.
One day tells its tale to another;
   and one night imparts knowledge to another.
Although they have no words or language;
   and their voices are not heard,
Their sound has gone out into all lands;
   and their message to the ends of the world. (Ps. 19:1–4)

Letting God Be God

Evangelist Luis Palau tells a story about his own encounter with Major W. Ian Thomas, a Christian evangelist and founder of Torchbearers International:[30]

> At one chapel service, he [Major Thomas] talked about how it took Moses forty years in the wilderness to learn that he was nothing all by himself. Then one day Moses was confronted with a burning bush. Likely a dry bunch of ugly sticks, yet Moses was instructed to take off his sandals. Why? Because God was in the bush!
>
> Major Thomas said, "God was telling Moses, 'I don't need a pretty bush or an educated bush or an eloquent bush. Any old bush will do as long as I'm in the bush. If I'm going to use you, it won't be you doing something for me, but me doing something through you."[31]

Luis Palau went on to realize he was that kind of bush—a useless bunch of dried-up sticks—and could do nothing for God. All his reading, study, planning, and modeling himself after others was worthless unless God was in the bush. Only he could make something happen. It was not about what Luis was going to do for God, but what God was going to do through Luis. He needed to let God be God.

Discipleship means letting go of those familiar and safe circumstances that keep God consigned to time-honored mantelpieces in our lives. We can be agents of change and we can make a difference, but ultimately we can't do anything for God. It is God working in us that does something in the world. We are not privy to where God is ultimately going at any given moment; we can only see where God has been. The rest becomes faith and trust in the unknown and unknowable persistence of God.

When we find ourselves in circumstances we don't choose, want, or understand, God might be working some purpose in us that we will only really see in hindsight. We have no guarantees of success, let alone how we might measure success. There is no angelic GPS device showing us the correct pathway. We most likely won't even know when we get to where God calls us because God will always

---

30 Torchbearers International is an organization that consists of more than twenty-six Bible schools and educational centers around the world.

31 "The Abundant Life Testimony of Luis Palau," www.gracenotebook.com/pub/534. html, accessed August 26, 2016.

be out in front calling us to the next place we are needed—always onward.

Bishop William Willimon from the United Methodist Church says:

> Faith, when it comes down to it, is our often breathless attempt to keep up with the redemptive activity of God, to keep asking ourselves, "What is God doing, where on earth is God going now?"[32]

There were many times when the disciples probably wondered that as well. It is the story of God's presence all through Scripture in the lives of women and men who didn't always know how their personal story would turn out. They could only be ordinary people witnessing to an extraordinary God. The stories they lived into became the possibilities through which God moved.

Three such stories are considered in this chapter. Peter is one character who is always being surprised by God. As the fledgling Christian church faced internal and external issues, Peter's exclamation of, "Who was I that I could hinder God!" is witness to the power of God. The Christmas story of Joseph's encounter with "angelic encouragement" reflects just one of the ways God was hidden in plain sight throughout the familiar and well-beloved Christmas stories. Thirdly, Peter and Paul were both transformed by God's compassion not in ways they expected, but in ways they needed. God continues to be predictably unpredictable by touching individual lives with surprises that heal brokenness, restore hope, and renew faith.

Our God has been a God of surprises for a very long time and there is not much we can do to change that. It seems to be the nature of God to continually lean into the future and encourage us to come along. Let us not be afraid, then, to let God be God.

---

32 William Willimon, *Acts: Interpretation: A Bible Commentary for Preaching and Teaching* (Louisville, KY: John Knox Press, 1988), 99.

CHAPTER 12

The God of Surprises

A Story of Peter and Cornelius

Reflect: When have you been surprised by God?

Read: Acts 10:1—11:18

E VERY YEAR FOR the few weeks following Easter, we hear the readings from the Acts of the Apostles, which contains stories of the formation of the early church. We have much to learn from it year after year, for many of the experiences they had we also have in the current Church: fierce arguments and disagreements about how things are supposed to be done; who is in and who is out; discovering unanticipated problems along the way and figuring out how to address them faithfully; wondering where God's Spirit is leading.

We read these stories so often we can lose the tremendous impact of what was really going on. These stories not only teach us about how the early church grew up but also how the Spirit of God worked in the lives of these early Jewish spiritual pioneers. By affiliation, we can ask, "How is the Spirit of God working in our own lives and times?"

The two chapters of Acts 10 and 11 tell the famous story of Peter the Apostle and Cornelius the Roman centurion (who also became the first non-Jewish convert). Peter and Cornelius represent two different life stories that came together in a surprising way: that of an apostle (who was Jewish) and that of a Roman official (a Gentile). The convergence of these two lives was where the powerful action of

God moved the early church to discern that God's grace was meant for all humankind, not just one small sect of Judaism.

Cornelius was what we would call today a "spiritual seeker." As a soldier in the Roman Empire, he had experience, discipline, and a keen sense of responsibility. He lived with his household in Caesarea, which was the local capital of that particular Roman province, Judea. He is described as being very devout—a man of constant prayer. He is also described as being a "God fearer." That was a term used to describe Gentiles who were drawn to the one God of the Jews but did not convert to Judaism. Instead, they attended synagogue, practiced some Jewish spiritual customs, and were sustained by a belief in the One God rather than the many gods of the Roman religious institution.[33]

Cornelius has had an angelic visitation in which he is told to send for a certain Simon, also called Peter, who is staying in Joppa, a town about thirty or so miles up the coast—two days' travel. Cornelius sends an envoy—a devout soldier along with two slaves—to Joppa to find this mysterious person.

In Roman culture, one's household included immediate family members as well as extended family and slaves. "Gentile" was a term to describe those who were not Jewish.

Peter, who is actually staying in Joppa with a friend, has no idea what is coming. He, too, has had a vision from God where God is presenting him with food and inviting him to eat it. However, this food consists of items that any faithful Jewish person would consider unclean to eat; yet in this vision, God persistently tells him three times to eat this food and says to Peter: "What God has made clean, you must not call profane" (Acts 10:15b).

This was a puzzling vision because it would have meant going against some of the most important traditions and teachings that Peter had learned since he was a small boy growing up in the Jewish faith. It would even have been going against how Jesus behaved when he was alive on earth. The riddle in this dream about eating unclean food left Peter perplexed when, unexpectedly, the envoy from Cornelius arrived at his doorstep.

It sounds as though Peter did not puzzle it out right away, for

---

33 William Barclay, *The New Daily Study Bible: The Acts of the Apostles* (Louisville, KY: Westminster John Knox Press, 2003), 91–92.

Luke[34] writes that God's Spirit had to tell Peter to get up and go with them to Cornelius's household. God had sent them to Peter and he was not to make a distinction between Jew and Gentile. It was pretty daring of Peter to obey and go since he was intentionally breaking all sorts of prohibitions in his culture and he knew it.

When he and his companions arrive at the household, Cornelius tells him about *his own* dream where he was told to send for Peter. Now, Cornelius wants to know what it is that God has commanded Peter to say to him. One can only wonder what went through Peter's thinking at this request from a Roman centurion. There is only one thing, however, that Peter can speak about with assurance, so he tells Cornelius and his household the story about Jesus: his life, his death, his resurrection, his appearances, his commandment to tell others the Good News.

This is the point at which God stirred the pot:

> While Peter was still speaking, the Holy Spirit fell upon all who heard the word. The circumcised believers [Peter's Jewish companions] who had come with Peter were astounded that the gift of the Holy Spirit had been poured out *even on the Gentiles*, for they heard them speaking in tongues and extolling God. Then Peter said, "Can anyone withhold the water for baptizing these people who have received the Holy Spirit just as we have?" So he ordered them to be baptized in the name of Jesus Christ. Then they invited him to stay for several days. (Acts 10:44–48)

Now, later in this story, when Peter returns to Jerusalem, he is confronted by his Jewish-Christian colleagues who want him to account for breaking one of the defining Jewish orthodoxies of the day. Didn't he know entering the household of Gentiles was prohibited? What was he thinking by hobknobbing and eating meals with those unclean outcasts? It is not until Peter describes his astounding experience that the others are swayed into acknowledging that something new might just be happening.

Peter explains:

> "And as I began to speak, the Holy Spirit fell upon them just as it had upon us at the beginning. And I remembered

---

34 While authorship of Acts is never clearly stated in the work itself, scholarship suggests that a Gentile-Christian by the name of Luke was the writer for both the Gospel of Luke and the Acts of the Apostles.

the word of the Lord, how he had said, 'John baptized with water, but you will be baptized with the Holy Spirit.' If then God gave them the same gift that he gave us when we believed in the Lord Jesus Christ, who was I that I could hinder God?" When they heard this, they were silenced. And they praised God saying, "Then God has given even to the Gentiles the repentance that leads to life." (Acts 11:15–18)

"Who was I that I could hinder God" is such a powerful observation not only for Peter, but for the early church as well, as they were struggling with that very issue of who was "in" and who was "out." Peter was not called to be the gatekeeper for God; he was called to pay attention to the cutting edge of the Spirit that was right in front of him. If Peter had played by the rules and not gone to see Cornelius, I have full confidence that the Spirit of God would have worked the message of inclusion through someone else. "God will get what God wants."

In the moment of confronting Peter for his maverick decision, however, I imagine more than one of Peter's colleagues asking the very question put forth by Bishop Willimon: "Where on earth is God going now?" It is intriguing to think of that question being asked over and over again across the millennia by so many saints and sinners who have come before us, as though it were some sort of new question.

The paths of these two lives, Peter and Cornelius, converged two thousand years ago, enabling the love of God to propel the early church into new territory that broadened its impact. It was unexpected. It was out of the ordinary. It broke the rules of the day, but it had the hidden fingerprints of God all over it.

I wonder where else might God be at work when two life paths converge? Unlike Robert Frost's poem "The Road Not Taken,"[35] it is not a choice of which path to take where the road divides, but rather, to seek the hand of God at work where the paths converge. Sometimes that merging becomes a positive link, such as that for Peter and Cornelius. Sometimes that convergence is not innately good, which makes it more difficult to perceive the hand of God at work.

Malala Yousafzai was a young advocate for education, especially for girls, in Pakistan. At age fifteen, her life path converged with that of a member of the Taliban who was intent on shutting down her voice

---

35 Robert Frost, "The Road Not Taken," http://www.poetryfoundation.org/poem/173536, accessed April 9, 2016.

for education: he shot her in the head while she traveled on a bus with some of her schoolmates. While a tragic incident all by itself, her amazing recovery and continued passion for the education of girls in developing nations led to her being awarded the Nobel Peace Prize in 2014 at the age of seventeen. She then founded The Malala Fund, which "has become an organization that, through education, empowers girls to achieve their potential and become confident and strong leaders in their own countries."[36] Two different paths converged. A tragedy took place and yet, something life-changing took hold in the world for thousands of young women. Their future, and the future of their children, will be constructively shaped by literacy and education. Multiple communities and countries will benefit from the leadership of these women both locally and globally. How could such an amazing story not have God's hand at work in it?

One cannot help but wonder how the life trajectory for the Taliban shooter might have been changed as well. Of course, we will probably never know the answer to that question; however, the apostle Paul, who was the most feared persecutor of Christians in the early church, had his life turned upside down by the surprise of the Holy Spirit. He went on to become one of the most influential and prominent Christian leaders in the expansion of the early Christian church, much to his own astonishment, I would imagine.

What potential do our own life convergences hold for change and promise? What thorny issues in today's world that seem so hopeless are prime subjects for a few God surprises? Where might God already be at work in your own story and those you meet in your everyday routine?

Humanity has a lot of experience with God doing pioneering things in our world and in our lives. It is almost as though seeking the growing edge of cultural norms is a key part of the way God works—even though it might not be the path we would naturally choose ourselves.

Like Peter and Cornelius, it is the surprises of God that catch us up breathlessly and propel us into unknown, unfamiliar, and sometimes unwelcome territory. The stealth of God is only recognized as we look through the rearview mirror of time; yet God plays for keeps and never seems to tire from seeking us out and finding us no matter where our paths have wandered. After all, who are we to hinder God?

---

36 "Malala Yousafzai—Biographical," October 19, 2016, www.nobelprize.org/nobel_prizes/peace/laureates/2014/yousafzai-bio.html, accessed August 30, 2016.

Connecting with Peter

Make a script out of the story from the Acts of the Apostles 10–11:18. The language lends itself easily to scripting. Locate some garments for costumes (capes, jackets, hats, shawls, boas, robes, vestments, uniforms, large pieces of fabric) and some items for props (bells, pretend swords, a sheet, stuffed animals, gaudy jewelry, military gear). Assign parts, particularly: Peter, Cornelius, the Holy Spirit, members of Cornelius's household, those who accompanied Peter and witnessed what happened, and the church leaders in Jerusalem who confronted Peter.

Consider the following questions in developing a personality for each character or group of characters: What is your character's background? Where did they grow up and what was their spiritual journey like? How did they wind up in the story? What is your character's motivation? What surprised them? What changed for them? How comfortable was that change? (It is okay to make some of this up. Try to be consistent with what we might already know from Scripture, however.)

After you play out the story, discuss what it felt like to be the various characters.

Speaking through the personality of your character, what do you think about Peter's comment, "If then God gave them the same gift that he gave us when we believed in the Lord Jesus Christ, who was I that I could hinder God?"

Pondering

What does it mean to hinder God? Is God's ongoing story being obstructed in today's world? If so, what does that look like? If God's actions cannot be thwarted, what does that mean for us?

The story of Peter and Cornelius is described as a "convergence" or conjunction of two life stories that led to a critical shift in the development of the early church. What other stories of "holy convergence" have you seen or experienced in others? What potential do our own path convergences hold for change and promise? Where might God be at work in these stories?

CHAPTER 13

Hidden in Plain Sight

A Story of Joseph, Jesus's Stepdad

Reflect: Have you ever been asked by God to do something unusual?

Read: Matthew 1:18–25

IT WAS CHRISTMAS Eve. A man was waiting for a bus to take him from Athens, Georgia, to Greenville, South Carolina. As he purchased his ticket, the agent said, "That bus is running a little late. If you'll just watch the electronic letter board over there in the corner, you will know when the bus arrives and when it's time to board."

The man wandered around the terminal for a while. Eventually he saw a small machine. The sign on the machine read, "For twenty-five cents, this machine will tell you your name, age, city of residence, and something about you."

"That's impossible," the man muttered out loud, but nevertheless he was curious, so he pulled out a quarter and plunked it into the machine. The machine whirred and whistled a bit, and then printed out a message that read: "Your name is Fred Jones. You are thirty-five years old. You live in Athens, Georgia, and you are waiting for a bus to Greenville, South Carolina."

"Incredible," said the man. "How does that machine know all of that? It's amazing, but I'll bet it can't do it again." So he plunked in another quarter. Again, the machine whirred and whistled for a bit, and then out came the message: "Your name is Fred Jones. You are thirty-five years old. You live in Athens, Georgia, and you are still waiting for a bus to Greenville, South Carolina."

"This cannot be happening!" the man exclaimed. He put on some sunglasses, mussed his hair a bit, turned the collar up on his jacket, and tried another quarter. The response came back: "Your name is still Fred Jones. You are still thirty-five years old. You still live in Athens, Georgia, and for the third time, you are still waiting for a bus to Greenville, South Carolina."

The man was amazed. He glanced across the street and saw a novelty shop. He walked out of the bus terminal, crossed the street, and went into the store. There he bought a pair of glasses with a large nose attached, a shaggy gray wig, a baggy shirt, and a cane. He then hobbled back across the street, acting like a much older man, and walked up to the machine. He put a fourth quarter into the slot. The machine whirred and groaned and whistled, and then put out a message that read: "Your name is Fred Jones. You are thirty-five years old. You live in Athens, Georgia; and while you were horsing around, you missed your bus to Greenville, South Carolina!"[37]

How human it was for Fred Jones to not quite believe his eyes, to be puzzled, to have a hard time trusting what he was seeing and hearing. It didn't fit his expectations. It was outside the realm of his experience, something different that didn't quite fit with the reality to which he was accustomed. He got lost in the details of trying to figure it out rather than getting lost in the wonder.

We don't have to look too far to identify with the tendency human beings have to get distracted in minutiae and "miss the bus," figuratively speaking, especially during the holiday season. Christmas is a paradox. Oh, most of us easily get caught up in the gift giving, the hustle and bustle, wrapping, decorating, the special music and performances that go along with this season, but at its heart, Christmas is a paradox: a god of power and might finding refuge in a feed trough, and angelic messengers who don't seek out the rich and famous, just shepherds minding their own business keeping careful watch over their sheep—one of the lowliest occupations of the day. Yet they are the ones who encounter the mystery, majesty, and awe of God on the loose. A package of human frailty not much bigger than a generous loaf of bread whose life, death, and resurrection was intended to put us in a living relationship with Divine Love.

---

37 James W. Moore, "Man in the Bus Terminal," in *The Miracle of Christmas: An Advent Study for Adults* (Nashville: Abingdon Press, 2006), 17–18. Used with permission.

Then there is the Holy Family: Mary—pregnant and unwed—stuck between a rock and a hard place. Joseph—wanting to quietly distance himself from her embarrassing situation—is the one who needs a bit of angelic convincing to finally pay attention to God at work in his life. Both plucked out of obscurity and simple lives. Each of them surprised by God and called unexpectedly to play a unique role in the history of the world. Remember also the Magi, traveling miles across foreign lands following what they thought was their true destination only to find they were in the wrong place at the right time. They followed a star that influenced them only to realize the destination was beyond their control.

God was yearning for personal connection with his creation and chose a baby to deliver that message. Human vessels, so flawed, fragile, and prone to failure by their very nature, were chosen by God.

Yes, the Christmas Story is a great paradox of a God who is frequently hidden in plain sight, as Joseph discovered.

> When Joseph awoke from sleep, he did as the angel of the Lord commanded him; he took her as his wife, but had no marital relations with her until she had borne a son; and he named him Jesus. (Matt. 1:24–25)

There was a television series a few years ago called *In Plain Sight.* It was about two federal marshals who were partners in the witness protection program in Albuquerque, New Mexico. Each episode focused on a particular story about someone just coming under the protection of the Federal Witness Program. For those who enter the safety net of this program, the life they knew changes suddenly and dramatically. The past needs to be suddenly abandoned, while the future is a totally blank slate. They are given new identities and relocated geographically to a different part of the country. They are protected by federal marshals but can tell their story to no one, for their safety relies on remaining "hidden in plain sight." Living the normalcy of the everyday with new identities and locations proves to be their greatest safeguard. While safety might be accomplished, it is still a tremendous burden and emotional shift to be living in the world with one set of norms and expectations, and then suddenly have it turned upside down to live according to an entirely different set of expectations.

That might have been part of Joseph's experience when he learned of the scandal that his betrothed wife was pregnant and it wasn't his child. As with many of our favorite Bible stories, there is significant drama going on behind the familiar tale in which, year after year, we know that everything turns out with a happy ending. But the "happy ending" was not at all apparent to either Joseph or Mary. We need to dig into the drama a bit and avoid the temptation to cover it up right away with soothing images, a dusting of angel glitter, and a bit of choir music humming in the background, because it is in the midst of the human drama where God is frequently hidden in plain sight.

Joseph is an unsung hero in the overall Christmas story. There is usually more focus on Mary and the babe in the manger than on the human to whom God entrusted their safety. While the Christmas stories are found exclusively in the two Gospels of Matthew and Luke, the particular story in Matthew 1:18–25 describes Joseph's encounter with the shocking and unwelcome news of perceived deception, disappointment of plans gone astray, betrayal by one who is beloved, and shame that would soon be making the rounds of the gossipmongers in the community.

Mary and Joseph were betrothed. This was the second step as a couple moved toward marriage. According to the custom of that time and culture, a betrothed couple was regarded as legally married, although they usually did not live together or have intimate relations until after the actual marriage celebration a year later. The only way to dissolve the union at this point was through divorce.[38]

When Joseph became aware that Mary was with child, he was within his rights to feel he had been deceived. This was not what he bargained for, not what he had committed to with Mary. The ball was now in his court and he had three choices he could make: He could just go through with the marriage, pretend nothing had happened and look like he had been premature in getting Mary pregnant before they were fully married. It was not the truth, but it would save face. Secondly, he could call her out and accuse her of adultery. This, of course, would possibly lead to her death by stoning, the custom for those caught in adultery (as it still is in some parts of the world today). But it was pretty cruel and he would have to live with the result of that decision the rest of his life. Finally, he could just divorce ("dismiss") her quietly. All he would need were two witnesses and to give her a letter divorcing her. This would preserve his dignity as

---

38 William Barclay, *The New Daily Study Bible: The Gospel of Matthew, Vol. 1* (Louisville, KY: Westminster John Knox Press, 2001), 22–23.

well as her life, was not avoiding the issue, and would set them both free to pursue their own lives apart from each other.

Joseph is described as being a righteous and just man, so this last option is the choice he made. He would quietly end the relationship—until an angel got in the way with new information. How could Joseph have possibly known that what was hidden in plain sight was God entering into a love affair with creation in an unexpected, if not slightly scandalous, way?

Now Joseph was a good choice for this role of earthly father for Jesus. He is believed to have been a carpenter and, like many craftsmen, he would have had the eye of an artist—seeing in an unwieldy block of wood the arm for a chair, or from the heart of a tree a bowl to hold food. Joseph knew how to follow the undiscovered purpose that the wood called forth while participating in the delight of creation. Due to this craftsmanship, Joseph probably had innate skills of perception, insight, and persistence. However, it took an angelic visitation for Joseph's eyes to be opened to the possibility that, like the wood with which he was familiar, there was something deeper going on. Something was calling him to tune in on a different internal frequency: to see the radical nature of God that was there all the time when no one else could or would see it; to shape and build a life for Mary and this child for whom he, Joseph, would be a protector and guardian; and to walk into the unknown future, much like his ancestor Abraham, as the hands and heart offered up to God's bigger story.

As the pieces of this deeply moving human drama gradually came together, a picture emerged. Not of being deceived by a faithless woman, but of being quietly invited into a partnership with a God who was hidden in plain sight all the time. One just needed to have the eyes to see and ears to hear. Like the scales that fell from Saul's eyes in his conversion experience, the denial of Peter foretold by Jesus, or the "Aha!" moments that occasionally show up in our own lives, sometimes it is the tiniest twist of fate that enables us to recognize what was there all along. Our reality doesn't change, but our perception of that reality does shift and becomes infused with greater meaning.

I had that experience a few years ago when I was serving a church as the assistant rector. A parishioner was preparing to move to China with her family. They would be gone for several years. Her name is Darcy and she gave me permission to tell her story.

Darcy is an unpretentious person, quick to offer a smile, laughter, and friendship. She does not stand out but kind of blends in easily. If she were in your congregation, you would find her quietly working in the kitchen, offering to ring the tower bell for any special occasion, or organizing festive receptions on Christmas Eve and Easter. Darcy would frequently take on tasks with which others did not want to be bothered.

Her most outstanding service to God's ministry in that congregation was the role she played in the development of food ministries. She just kept moving quietly forward from one thing to the next: sometimes helping out with existing food programs like senior luncheons and Salvation Army dinners; sometimes starting new initiatives like her frozen casserole ministry—all because she saw a need. She was always on the hunt for how she could help the hungry in new ways.

As Darcy and I began having conversation about how to transition her various leadership roles to others prior to her leaving for China, I realized that God was "hidden in plain sight" in her ministry. Darcy embodied the heart of a deacon, much like those who were called in the early church to serve the poor, the hungry, the widows, and the orphans.

You don't have to wear a clerical collar to be called and ordained by God to ministry. Darcy might not have been ordained in the same way that most clergy are, but God had certainly called and ordained her to a ministry of servanthood, one that is still affirmed by all who know her and work alongside her, even in China.

Quietly and unknowingly, God showed up and called Darcy. She responded and God's work in Shelburne, Vermont, took shape in a food ministry that continues to feed the hungry. Her work became a sacrament: an "outward and visible sign of inward and spiritual grace."[39]

She had choices. She could have said, "I have no time," and gone on her way. She could have ignored those moments of need that crossed her path. There is a range of responses that Darcy or any one of us could make in such circumstances. Like Joseph, who initially made the choice to dismiss Mary quietly and get on with his life, we are faced with a range of responses to what God might be calling us to be and do in our individual or communal lives. We can dismiss those moments quietly, let them pass and return to the familiar. We can

---

39 BCP, 857.

name them publicly and then look around for someone else to do something; or we can step outside of our comfort zone, trust God, and see what happens. It is not our job to second-guess God at work. It is our job to look, listen, learn, and respond when and where we can. God will do the rest.

To follow God into the unknown might just find us pricked by wonder like Joseph, Mary, the shepherds, the Magi, and even those unknown witnesses to the birth story like the innkeeper and his wife. We are not all that much different from those whose stories we hear every year: the shepherds, minding their own business; the innkeeper, shooing people away from his door and not wanting to be bothered; the Holy Family, not quite sure where all this was going. We come seeking. We come out of curiosity. We come carrying our load of worry, anxiety, and fear. We come living the question of how to move forward into the future when parts of the future might seem so uncertain. And into that quandary, we find the hope of God at work: the shepherds, lost in wonder and amazement; the innkeeper, finally touched with compassion and responding with help; the Holy Family, trusting God and walking into the unknown because they knew God would be there with them.

And ourselves? Well, I suppose that part of God's story is still being written. We follow the star and the story not because they are cute and simple, but because they are profound and life-changing. God's relentless love is always revealing something to get our attention so that we might turn around and find our Creator. And we do. We all take different paths to seek the manger, but eventually we find it brimming with the light of the world dwelling in human hearts.

It is a grand adventure to keep tabs on this God who is radically hidden in plain sight. Well, perhaps it is not we who need to keep tabs on God, but God who keeps tabs on us. For in the midst of our human predisposition, we are easily sidetracked by life's distractions.

> "Do not be afraid, Joseph," said the angel. "For the child in Mary's womb is from the Holy Spirit. She will bear a son and you are to name him Jesus—Emmanuel—which means, 'God *is* with us.'" (Matt. 1:20–23, paraphrase)

God *is* with us. Not God *was* with us in a sweet little story that happened nearly two thousand years ago. God is in our past, our present, and our future and that changes everything, so we need not be afraid. Jesus revealed the hand of God from the time he was in the womb. He is God's way of saying: "Ready or not, here I am."

Connecting with Joseph

You are a carpenter and, according to some accounts, you might have been a widower, making this betrothal to Mary a possible marriage of convenience for you—someone to take care of you as you grow older. The companionship might be nice. She seems to be a nice girl. Her family is certainly supportive of this agreement and you won't be alone so much. The problem is that this little arrangement is not going quite the way you had imagined. You have always lived your life quietly, even shyly. Following the rules, not making waves or causing disturbances, and now here you are faced with the possibility that you are actually marrying a very young girl who is carrying someone else's child. That is unheard of and will push your quiet self out into the open more than you want. How to counter the gossiping neighbors who will inevitably get wind of this? How do you really feel about raising someone else's child? What did that powerful "dream" mean? It was more like a vision because it was so real. The angel's message was so on target with what you were feeling and getting ready to do by dismissing Mary and ending this betrothal.

What does Joseph's struggle feel like? What is the hardest part of Joseph's turmoil? What does it feel like to consider the idea that God has reached out to you personally? What does it stir in you to realize you might well have exactly what God needs at this moment in time to advance that which God wants to do?

Pondering

Think of a time when an assumption you had made about God or God's actions turned out to be different from what you had imagined. What was "hidden in plain sight"? Did your intuition open up a new reality? Did God seem to be any part of that?

CHAPTER 14

When Love Came to Town

A Story of Peter, Paul, and Alyssa

Reflect: Where is God at work in you?
Read about Peter: John 21:1–17
Read about Paul: Acts 9:1–20

WASHINGTON NATIONAL CATHEDRAL in Washington, DC, is one of my favorite places to visit. One of the most famous Episcopal churches in the country, you may recognize it from mentions in the news as the National Cathedral, but its real name is The Cathedral Church of St. Peter and St. Paul.

Two stunning stone carvings over the front door of the cathedral hold together two great leaders of the Christian Church: Peter, the great fisherman whose story of commissioning by Christ is told in the Gospel of John, and Paul, the great evangelist to the Gentiles whose conversion story is found in the book of Acts.

Peter and Paul: one a simple fisherman, probably illiterate, a direct disciple of Jesus; the other an educated, connected Roman citizen. Both Jewish. Both zealous. Both coming from different lifestyles and life experiences, but both called by the risen Christ to begin again when they thought all was lost to them. Both became dynamos in the early church because Love came to town seeking them out.

Let's take a look at Peter's story first. The story in Scripture (referred to above) takes place shortly after Jesus's resurrection.

This was the third time Jesus had appeared to the disciples after his death. We don't know Peter's frame of mind at this point, but it is probably safe to say that a bit of confusion was in the minds of each of the disciples. Peter does what many of us do when we need some mental space while chewing on thorny issues—he gets busy with his brawn rather than his brain and turns to a familiar touchstone. He goes fishing with some of the other disciples, most likely to provide some food and money to support themselves for the time being. They didn't expect Jesus to make a surprise appearance on the beach, but there he was instructing them to toss their nets to the other side of the boat, where they successfully pulled in dozens of fish even though there had been nothing caught in their nets all night long. That miracle had echoes of miracles they had seen in the past—feeding the multitudes and water that was turned into the finest wine—abundance where there only seemed to be scarcity before.

Jesus's unexpected appearance to them on the beach gently confronts Peter with the failure of his lifetime: his denial of Jesus during those last horrible days of Jesus's life. Jesus foretold that Peter would deny him and, in spite of Peter's heated response of "Even though I must die with you, I will not deny you" (Matt. 26:35), denial is exactly what he did—three times—as Jesus predicted. Peter carried this shame and guilt with him and, as with most things we are ashamed of, we cannot see it on the surface, although its weight can be like an albatross around one's neck.

Well, Jesus tends to see those things we carry around and try to hide. He speaks to Peter's hidden, broken heart when he asks three times: "Peter, do you love me?" Peter responds with, "Yes, LORD—you know I love you." Jesus responds, "Then, feed my sheep, tend my lambs."

This threefold ritual mirrors Peter's threefold denial. Who would ever see Peter as the rightful leader after his clear denial of even knowing Jesus, yet here was Jesus restoring him and commissioning him to carry on in Jesus's place. Jesus still trusted Peter and still saw his worth. He still wanted Peter to continue caring for his flock.

God's boldness forgave, renewed, and restored Peter to wholeness. Peter went on to become one of the premier leaders of the early Christian church.

When Love came to town, it had Peter's name on it.

Now, let's turn our attention for a minute to Paul, the other apostle on the carving over the door at the National Cathedral.

Paul's original name was Saul. He was Jewish but not one of the twelve at all. He never met Jesus while Jesus was alive; never heard him teach or saw him do a miracle; was probably nowhere near the crucifixion at the time. Saul might have heard about Jesus as word spread about this upstart Jewish splinter group in the community. As a faithful Jew, he seemed to take it upon himself to rid the community of these upstarts and he became one of the most feared fanatics in the days of the early church. He went from house to house dragging off both men and women to prison, and then he went one step further. He approached the high priest in Jerusalem and asked for letters to the synagogues of Damascus so he might search for anyone there who were "Followers of the Way," as the original name given to the early followers of Jesus. He would arrest them and bring them to prison in Jerusalem. This is what put him on the road to Damascus in the first place and where the direction of his life changed forever.

Saul/Paul: the proud and passionate persecutor of those who were "Followers of the Way" was bound up in his self-perception as God's appointed instrument of justice and religious cleansing. Saul was knocked flat by a light from heaven speaking to him, "Why are you persecuting me?" He became temporarily blinded by that event and while he was lying helpless and blind, hoping that he might miraculously heal, he might have asked himself a thousand times: "Why did this happen? I'm a good person, a messenger of God. What has gone wrong? How can I get out of this?" Ananias—one of those whom Saul had been seeking to persecute—was rather hesitant to make himself known to Saul, who still had the fierce reputation of persecuting Christians. But Ananias healed him.

Saul's life direction turned around dramatically and, along with changing his name to Paul, he went from being an agent of death and persecution to being God's instrument of spreading God's Good News to a wider audience outside Jewish territory. His zealous fanaticism became something God would use, but only after Paul gave up the person he thought he was supposed to be in order to become the person God needed him to be.

When Love came to town, it had Paul's name on it.

The touch of Love is not limited to these stories from ancient writings, however. A few years ago, my dental hygienist, Alyssa, shocked me speechless when I politely asked her the usual niceties, "Anything new with you since I last saw you six months ago?" and she responded, "Well, yes. I found God."

Now, for a priest in a dental office, that is a showstopper; for a minute my mouth hung open, but not for her to start cleaning my teeth! I asked to hear her story and she likewise gave me permission to use it here. She described a recent time that had been a very dark journey for her: her brother in rehab for heroin addiction, her own recent divorce, and a consequent move to a new apartment. It sounded like one of those times many of us experience in life when things just cave in on multiple fronts and we are literally driven to our knees. She had just read *The Cross and the Switchblade* by David Wilkerson with John and Elizabeth Sherrill[40] and some verses from Psalm 31 spoke directly into her life:

> Have mercy on me, O LORD, for I am in trouble; my eye is consumed with sorrow, and also my throat and my belly. For my life is wasted with grief, and my years with sighing; my strength fails me because of affliction, and my bones are consumed. . . . I am forgotten like a dead man, out of mind; I am as useless as a broken pot (Ps. 31:9–10, 12 NRSV)

She described that her life felt like shards of pottery trying to be held together when it was broken open with a flood of tears, sorrow, seeking, and praying to Jesus for help. What happened next is one of those circumstances that I can only describe as moments of grace when the Holy Spirit shows up unexpectedly with amazing comfort.

As she was sitting alone after the storm of tears had subsided a bit, she became aware of three small lights in her peripheral vision that drew her attention, not to mention her curiosity. As she described it to me, she looked at them, but they multiplied and surrounded her and for what seemed like several minutes, she said, "it was like being surrounded by glitter" before they faded away. But she knew she had been found by God's love in a way that she would never have predicted, let alone understood. She described herself as "being saved" and I believe that is true. Her life was restored, renewed, and redirected in a new way, as was her brother's life and that of her parents. I didn't ask her if she now went to church. I didn't want to know. Somehow it seemed as though that question might take away the impact of the

---

40 *The Cross and the Switchblade* (New York: Penguin Publishing, 1962) is about Pastor Wilkerson's work with gangs in NYC. The impact of that ministry has included the development of "Teen Challenge," a spiritually based recovery program with a high success rate in working with addictions in youth.

story because truly, when Love came to town, it had Alyssa's name on it and "church" had nothing to do with it.

Peter. Paul. Alyssa. There is no going back when God's love finds you.

God shone Christ's light into their personal darkness. God led them to something new that they didn't expect but which was exactly what they needed: a way of life that is not content with things as they are, but sees things as they can be—life where there is death. Hope where there is despair. Trust where there is betrayal. A gentle touch where there is need for healing. It is a resurrection way of life.

When Love comes to town, it comes with each of our names on it, but we don't always see it. Sometimes, it can be pretty dramatic like Alyssa's or Paul's stories. Sometimes, it kind of glides into your normal everyday, like Peter, who was able to move beyond his shame to know that Love had found him more deeply than before. There would be no going back to life fishing in the sea. He went on to become a great fisherman of men and women.

Paul went on to become a great evangelist and founder of new churches among the non-Jewish population. Allysa is still moving forward in her own journey with God in the mix. Who knows where that will lead?

The work of Easter is never finished.

> We are invited to start over. We are completely loved. And we have a job to do. This isn't only Peter's story [or Paul's story or Alyssa's]; it's our story, too. When fear holds us back, love calls us forward. When we feel trapped by the way things have always been, Jesus invites us to cast our nets on the other side of the boat—change our perspective. . . . The light of resurrection, shining into us, invites us to look clearly at how we have made choices out of fear rather than love, and to move away from the fears that bind us.[41]

As Luis Palau discovered at the beginning of this section, we can do nothing for God by ourselves, but God can do something with us all the time. We need to let God be God and hang on for the adventure.

---

41 Kay Sylvester, "The Work of Easter, 3 Easter (C)," *Sermons That Work,* April 14, 2013, http://episcopaldigitalnetwork.com/stw/2013/03/29/3-eater-c-2013/, accessed August 30, 2016.

Connecting with Peter

On the day Jesus was arrested, you and the other disciples were terrified for your lives. You ran to find out what happened to him but couldn't get too close. He was beyond a wall somewhere and the closest you could get without getting caught yourself was a huddle of people trying to keep warm around a fire. Did it catch you by surprise that you were recognized? Did your denial of even knowing him just explode out of your mouth before you remembered his prediction? Before you remembered you said you would die with him? What did you think when the cock crowed? Did you feel like a fool? A hypocrite? A fraud? A phony? How deep were your despair and shame after Jesus died? Did you ever think you could redeem yourself? Fast-forward to that day on the beach after the resurrection. The reality of the resurrection was something you and the others had begun to grasp. What was it like for Jesus to still hold out his heart to you and place his hope for the future in your very human hands? What changed in you from the day of your denial through the time of this event on the beach?

Connecting with Paul

Your animosity for the "Followers of the Way" was legendary before your own conversion experience. You were driven to purify the ranks of the Jews by eliminating those who claimed to be followers of Jesus and you were good at it. On your way to Damascus to hunt down Christians and drag them in chains to Jerusalem for trial, a great light blinded you and instead of entering Damascus in grim triumph, you had to be submissively led there by your friends, for your sight was gone and your confidence shattered. In your culture, a person who was blind or who became ill or lame was thought to have sinned against God in some way. Did this question haunt you during the three long, lonely days and nights in blindness? Had you somehow sinned by being faithful to your religion? Did the voice of Jesus that you heard leave you with some hard questions to ask yourself?

What was it like to have a stranger—Ananias—come help you? You didn't ask for him. You didn't even know him. He was one of those Christians who should be running from you. He said he came because God sent him to heal you. When your sight returned, you were a totally different person from a few days earlier. People didn't want to believe you had changed. What was it like to be lit up inside with a new light so bright you couldn't help but sing the new song that was in your heart? How do you explain what happened to you?

Pondering

What new thing is God doing in your life lately? What new spirit is being born in you? Is there a new song playing in your heart, a new longing yearning to be expressed? Where might God be at work in your own story?

PART FIVE

Trusting an Unknown Future to a Known God

Your word is a lantern to my feet
and a light upon my path. (Ps. 119:105)

Trusting an Unknown Future to a Known God

"Never be afraid to trust an unknown future to a known God"[42] is a quote by Corrie ten Boom that came my way while serving a local congregation as assistant rector. The national economic train wreck of 2008, in addition to the parish's struggle with income and expenses, forced the church to reexamine its budgetary priorities and my position was eliminated at the end of 2011. After eight and a half years of full-time service, it was a bit of a free fall following the previous summer's sabbatical that had been so grounding. Not only was it a loss of job and income, it was also a loss of a significant spiritual family with whom I enjoyed fellowship on Sunday mornings and throughout the week.

The idea of trusting my own unknown future to a God that doesn't quit was easier to say than to do. It was a comforting and daring idea; however, the reality of living into that kind of vague prospect felt more like falling off a cliff in the dark with no idea where the bottom was. Rarely have I had the experience of walking into a dark space feeling so alone, but the winter of 2011–2012 was exactly that. In hindsight, it was a time of tremendous spiritual growth, although it did not seem that way at the time. It was enough for me to try to get through each day with dignity, love, and grace. My own life story was still being seasoned in ways I had yet to accept.

Joy, loss, surprise, fear, and opportunity inevitably shape our lives. While we can't always control those situations, it seems that God works in a discreet partnership with us, creating good and loving outcomes in spite of ourselves.

The reflections offered in this chapter explore four different aspects of unknown futures: when individual and spiritual blindness generate from fear of change, the visible can become invisible. Can we actually see something familiar with new eyes? Can we possibly imagine that something else might be taking place that we didn't allow ourselves to see before?

Life often takes an unexpected turn—the landscape is no longer familiar and we find ourselves on an irreversible path that we didn't choose, but one with which we are forced to deal. We might resist making peace with the new situation, but we have now embarked on a journey to find a "new normal." How do we shift our perspective

---

42 Corrie ten Boom, www.goodreads.com/quotes/70125-never-be-afraid-to-trust-an-unknown-future-to-a, accessed August 30, 2016.

to consider that God might well be doing something new with our something old?

There is a very fine line of perception between a glass that is half full and a glass that is half empty. Unknown futures are that way as well, especially as the modern church tries to figure out where God is leading. Reframing the familiar to look through a different lens than the one we have been using might enable us to discover God at work in the unexpected, the untraditional, and the unconventional. Where are the surprising places the Holy is still luring us forward?

Lastly, like magnificent stained glass windows whose beauty only becomes evident when the light shines through them, our own stories are windows through which God shines light, love, compassion, challenge. So, too, is it with the stories of people from Scripture that we have been considering in this book.

God is always calling us regardless of any religious affiliation and is never short of ideas of how to get through our more stubborn human nature. It doesn't matter if we are aware of it in traditional ways or not, for "bidden or unbidden, God is still present."[43]

---

43 Desiderius Erasmus, www.azquotes.com/quote/427536, accessed August 30, 2016.

CHAPTER 15

Visible but Invisible

A Story of the Man Blind from Birth

Reflect: When have you discovered a "blindness" in yourself or others?

Read: John 9:1–38

I N THE CULTURE of Jesus's day, people who were blind, crippled, deaf, or had some disfiguring illness were cursed and treated as outcasts. They lived on the fringes of society, had to beg for money and food in order to just exist, and were seen but not really noticed by the public. People walked on by these other human beings every day. It is fair to say that individuals like the blind man in this Gospel story simply became an unnoticed part of the fabric of the town. They were visible, but invisible. They had their place and everyone believed, including the blind man, this was just the way the world worked. Perhaps God really *was* a vengeful being and the mystery of why he had been blind from birth would always remain an unanswered question. Surely, his blindness was not anything to show God's glory. It only showed to the world that this man or his parents had somehow sinned and incurred God's anger. No one saw fit to challenge that idea, until Jesus came along.

The blind man might not have his sight, but he had his other physical senses. He would have heard the crowds approaching and felt the energy they produced. With a lifelong sharpened sense of hearing, he would have focused on Jesus's voice and absorbed the meaning of his words. He would have sensed the movement of the individuals about him as people jockeyed for position around this teacher passing through town. He would have realized he had been spotted when some strange voices blurted out that repulsive question that singled him out as an object lesson yet again: "Rabbi, who sinned, this man or his parents, that he was born blind?" as though he could not hear them.

But this stranger, who was called Jesus, didn't use the blind man's condition as a moral lesson about sin and punishment. This teacher whom he could only hear and sense said something he hadn't heard before: "Neither this man blind since birth nor his parents had sinned. His blindness is a tool through which God would work and in which God's glory would be revealed."

This blind man who had spent his life being held up as a despised warning against sin finds himself treated with respect and not as a pariah, perhaps for the first time. He is honored as a person who yearns for life just like anyone else. God has chosen him to be the instrument through whom God's power and love will shine through to the community. That is certainly good news he has never heard before.

Jesus makes a bit of mud, wipes it on the man's eyes, and instructs him to go wash in the Pool of Siloam. He does so and his sight is miraculously restored. The man is not only given physical sight, but also a new reason to reconsider the purpose of his life.

The story doesn't end there, however. The newly sighted man, who is now able to appreciate colors, shapes, and features of all that he could not see before, is about to discover an aspect of community that always lies just under the surface of polite society: change is hard and no one likes it.

Like a mobile that hangs in perfect balance until you add or subtract one of its dangling pieces, changing one seemingly insignificant part of a community ripples throughout the entire body until a new state of equilibrium is achieved. Communities are not always ready or willing to see things in a different way. In some ways, they can be blind, too.

Some people couldn't believe anything had changed. They said: "Isn't this the man who used to sit and beg?" Others said: "No. Can't be. It's just someone who looks like him." Their disbelief was joined with the blindness of the Pharisees, who were more concerned that the ancient laws had been broken by performing a nonemergency ("elective") healing on the Sabbath. They were confused and conflicted, even among themselves, as to whether Jesus really could be from God. Some were saying that if he does not observe the Sabbath, how could he really be from God? Others challenged back saying, well how could someone perform such signs like this if he were not from God? They became more concerned about having an intellectual theological debate on the issue and apprehending the person who upset the status quo than they were in being amazed that a member of their community was now miraculously restored to new life in the neighborhood.

The Pharisees could not let go of the issue, so they dragged this man's parents before them and asked them: "Was this their son? Had he really been born blind? If so, how is it, then, that he now sees and who caused that to happen?" The parents, who were wisely afraid they would be driven out of the synagogue themselves, did a beautiful end run around the subject and answered: "Yes, he is our son. Yes, he was born blind. Yes, he apparently now sees. We have no idea how that happened, nor who did it. Ask him. He is a grown-up. He will speak for himself." Yet even that was not enough—the blind man was brought back for a second interview before the religious authorities during which the newly sighted man embarrassed the Pharisees with his own keen insight about their lack of vision.

Clearly, Jesus's intervention in this man's life caused quite a bit of turmoil; it really upset the apple cart in town. The religious leaders were not about to be lectured so perceptively by someone who was recently an outcast, so they said: "You were born entirely in sin, yet you are trying to teach us?"

So, the Pharisees did what insecure leadership has always done when someone speaks truth to power—they drove him out.

Not only were certain laws broken by healing on the Sabbath by some stranger no one could identify, who must be—but could not really be—from God, but also a blind man who could now see meant the community's perception and behavior had to change. They could no longer think of him in the same old way. The community did not realize that they were really the spiritually blind ones in need of healing. God might be doing something different from what they already knew and expected. The arrival of God's light into our world challenges and changes our comfortable perceptions.

In Shelburne, Vermont, there was a mobile home park called Shelburnewood that was located right behind the parking lot of

Trinity Episcopal Church. It was home to twenty-eight low-income families, hidden by the cedar trees that had been planted as a privacy hedge between the two properties. Most days it was easy to be like the Pharisees and neighbors of the blind man in this Gospel story. It was easy to not pay attention to the presence of the trailers and people who lived behind the parking lot. They seemed to be a part of the quiet fabric of the neighborhood. They were visible if we looked, but invisible because we were not really inclined to look.

In March 2005, all twenty-eight families were served with eviction notices. The mobile home park was closing and they had eighteen months to leave and find someplace else to live. This prime land was being sold to a developer for building a few very high-priced homes in the charming village portion of Shelburne. Twenty-eight families living in some of the limited affordable housing that existed in Shelburne would no longer be neighbors. Some of them had sunk everything they had into their mobile homes whose equity had already plummeted. Even if they could find a mobile home park somewhere in Vermont willing to take these aging mobile homes, they were no longer up to current building codes. In addition, some people would have to give up their jobs and find new employment elsewhere. Children would have to be uprooted from the local school. Hopes and dreams and, in some cases, life savings that had been invested in a place to live, were in danger of being flattened.

It is one of the foundational values of the Episcopal Church to say: "We will seek Christ in all persons; love our neighbor as ourselves; strive for justice and peace among all people and respect the dignity of every human being."[44] So, the people of Trinity Episcopal Church on the other side of the parking lot's cedar hedge had to consider what God might be calling them to be and do with the "visible but invisible" neighbors who lived behind the church.

It was the start of a long and arduous process of supporting the people of Shelburnewood through offering meeting space, listening to their individual stories, attending public meetings with them, helping make connections and build relationships in the town, and spreading the word to other influential parties. Over a million dollars was spent by one committed developer proposing an extensive design that would have enabled the people to stay in their homes as well as develop affordable housing, only to be continually shot down by town

---

44 BCP, 305, paraphrase.

officials for one reason or another. He finally gave up. Community supporters grew disheartened. The future of these vulnerable people seemed so bleak at times. Eventually, after eight long and discouraging years, philanthropist and real estate developer Tony Pomerleau of Burlington learned of their plight and stepped forward to purchase the property as an act of solidarity with the residents of Shelburnewood as well as for the development of affordable housing in the quaint village of Shelburne that was within walking distance of schools, shopping, churches, and town offices. Now under the management of the Cathedral Square Corporation,[45] this property currently includes affordable housing as well as apartments for seniors and people with disabilities.

The people of the original Shelburne Mobile Home Park have remained in place and have also formed a cooperative so they might own the land under their mobile homes. Significant improvements to lighting, energy, water, and road access have been included in the development of the entire property.

This repurposing of a mobile home park into a modern, affordable housing development was very much a joint effort by the people of Shelburnewood along with support by many others in the community, including leadership from the rector and members of Trinity Episcopal Church. It would have been so easy to remain blind to the plight of these neighbors hidden behind the cedar trees at the edge of the parking lot. Change and its prickly challenge to our comfort zone present both strain and opportunity. Frequently, they are a sign that the Holy Spirit is very much at work.

Jesus healed a man's blindness when and where he could. It didn't matter that it was a Sabbath day when no such work should be done. There was someone in need and he could do something about it. So he did. He asks the same of us.

The Pharisees in the story would never accept the kind of faithfulness that is measured by addressing justice and dignity. They would not be changed by evidence, nor could they afford to consider that they might be wrong. They were locked in to a vision that had rules but no compassion, a hard line but no common sense—a role of protecting the law that they fulfilled admirably, but didn't include

---

45 Vermont Elder Resource Group, "Cathedral Square Corporation," https://cathedralsquare.org/community-celebrates-new-neighborhood/, accessed August 30, 2016.

room for the unexpected interruption of God. The only blindness that didn't get healed in this story was theirs.

> The position of the man's accusers—the hardline Pharisees who are sticking to their principles at the cost of the evidence—is then all the more devastatingly exposed. Not only are they wrong, but they have constructed a system within which they will never see that they were wrong. It is one thing to be genuinely mistaken, and to be open to new evidence, new arguments, new insights. It is another to create a closed world, like a sealed room into which no light, no fresh air, can come from outside.[46]

There is a price for having one's blindness transformed. The price is that we can't go back and unlook or unknow what we were previously able to ignore. Like the Shelburnewood story, when Jesus comes into a person's life or a community's harmony, things are inevitably broken open, shaken up, and energized in new ways. Invisible faith becomes visible action whenever and wherever issues of dignity, respect, and justice are perceived differently from that of the status quo. God's dream moves a little closer to being fully realized in our world whenever unconditional love becomes the vehicle for mercy, compassion, dignity, and integrity toward those we meet along the way.

Connecting with the Man Blind from Birth

Certain words from the song "Amazing Grace" literally apply to you: "Once I was blind, but now I see." Was it frustrating to be a constant source of derision in the town due to your blindness? What did you think about the belief that somehow you or your parents had sinned, causing your blindness? What was it like to be given the gift of sight, but have no idea who had healed you because he was a stranger? Did the negative reaction and persistence of the Pharisees surprise you? What was so hard for them to believe? They eventually threw you out of the temple. Did you care? Did that mean anything to you at the moment? Jesus came and found you. What did you feel when you saw him for the first time?

---

46 N. T. Wright, *John for Everyone, Part 1, Chapters 1–10* (Louisville, KY: Westminster John Knox Press, 2004), 146.

Pondering

Some blindness seeks to be healed; some does not. What are some examples of spiritual blindness in which an individual does not realize he might be blind? What are some examples in our current culture of blindness that require healing? Where might God be already at work in that picture? Where might you be at work in that picture?

CHAPTER 16

Discovering the New Normal

A Story of Despair—A Story of Healing

Reflect: When have you cried out to God in joy? In despair?

Read: Psalm 40:1–14

I T IS EASY to pay scant attention to that which is familiar: the everyday routines we have, people we work alongside, things that bring us comfort. This path is familiar, comfortable, energizing in different ways, and it is uniquely ours. Life goes on day after day. Some new things happen. Some surprises come along from time to time, but overall we don't even notice how comforting our life can be until something about that journey changes and we find ourselves on a path not of our choosing. A loving partner in life dies. An unexpected illness intrudes. A disaster befalls us. An accident takes away what used to be. There is no longer any familiar territory. We become as strangers in a strange land without a road map, a compass, or even a sense of what to do next. Try as we might, we cannot go back to what was. It will never be ours again. There is no more "normal" as we knew it. Nothing has the look of normal at all. We might rage against the circumstances that brought us to this new place, but no matter how much we rail against it, we do not have the power to change it. Eventually, we unwillingly set out on a journey of searching for what will become our "new normal." Our quest is a psalm in progress.

The Psalms are an interesting collection of prayers, poems, and songs. They are not a specific life story per se as much as they are windows that allow us a peek into the laments, struggles, delights, sorrows, thanksgivings, and hopes of nameless authors in a setting that was most likely part of the worship life of ancient Israel.

Each was written by human hands and provoked by someone's life experience, whether that was a search for God, a cry for help, or a testimony of thanksgiving. They are portals into someone's unknown story. Study the following and ask yourself the question: "What was the author feeling?"

> When I consider your heavens, the work of your fingers, the moon and the stars you have set in their course, what is man that you should be mindful of him? The son of man that you should seek him out? (Ps. 8:4–5, BCP)

> LORD, you have searched me out and known me; you know my sitting down and my rising up; you discern my thoughts from afar. . . Where can I go then from your Spirit? where can I flee from your presence? (Ps. 139:1, 6, BCP)

> I remember you upon my bed, and meditate on you in the night watches. For you have been my helper, and under the shadow of your wings I will rejoice. (Ps. 63:6–7, BCP)

There is so much material in the Psalms that gives us pause to wonder: "What was going on that prompted this unknown person to write that verse? What was in their heart? What was their story?" In many cases, these ancient writers seem to be sharing part of their personal journey of searching for their own "new normal."

> My God, my God, why have you forsaken me? and are so far from my cry and from the words of my distress? O my God, I cry in the daytime, but you do not answer; by night as well, but I find no rest. (Ps. 22:1–2, BCP)

> My spirit faints within me; my heart within me is desolate. . . . I spread out my hands to you; my soul gasps to you like a thirsty land. . . . Let me hear of your loving kindness in the morning, for I put my trust in you; show me the road I must walk, for I lift up my soul to you. (Ps. 143:4, 6, 8, BCP)

Sometimes our own unique stories reflect a similar struggle, whether we can put it into words or not. Consider this account from the daily devotional booklet *Forward Movement Day by Day*:

> My sister was a busy art teacher, wife, and mother. Nine years ago, she was driving to her daughter's middle school basketball game one Friday afternoon when a truck jumped the median and hit her head-on. After the jaws-of-life and rescue helicopter, she was in the trauma unit for weeks and in rehab for months. After she came home, her husband remembered that the police had collected the items scattered at the accident scene. Hesitantly she went through them, finding, along with her cell phone, the "to-do" list she had intended to accomplish that weekend of the accident. Those things didn't get done. But she had lived, against the odds. She (and I) got a new perspective about plans. Following that, she read a book by a person who had received similar injuries and who wrote of accepting the "new normal." The challenge was to refuse to live in regret about how life might have been, about the "to-do" lists that could no longer include certain activities. As she embraced the idea of living in the "new normal," God put a "new song" in her mouth. The new song was courageous and beautiful.[47]

This story is a song of lament and a thanksgiving that was oddly shaped by a life event that could well crush someone's soul. The story is tragic but the ultimate outcome led her to a new landscape that she might never have discovered if her journey had not been so terribly disrupted. God was still there in her story, just as vibrant, just as loving, just as present as before, but now in a new way.

Life disruptions throw us all into a pit of despair at one time or another. The path we are on evaporates for one reason or another and we are left in limbo for a time. It is dark and strange. There is no map or GPS tool that clearly takes us from the old path into the ways of the new path. We have to face into the unknown. There is no choice. The loss can be overwhelming, the grief unbearable. New routines. New people. Where is that which we have loved for so long? Where did it go so quickly?

It is as though we have to stumble around in the dark for a time. It almost seems that this experience is part of the formula to find the

---

47 Ann Rose, *Forward Day By Day* 81, no. 1 (February 25, 2015), page 30.

outline of something familiar that we seek. We are on a new path that we do not recognize because we have not fully discovered it yet.

As the psalmists invoked so long ago, sometimes there is only one place to turn to for help in our darkest hours:

> Save me, O God, for the waters have risen up to my neck. I am sinking in deep mire, and there is no firm ground for my feet. . . . Answer me, O LORD, for your love is kind; in your great compassion, turn to me. (Ps. 69:1–2, 18, BCP)

A kind of wintry season of the soul sets in during these times. It seems to be a necessary step, allowing God's story in us to unfold uniquely and quietly at its own pace. Don't rush through it. Put down the burdens and just be present. One can hope and listen for the springlike stirrings of newness, but don't be in too much of a rush to get there. It will come when it—and you—are ready. There is much to be explored while allowing winter to teach about patience and faith in the future. What has been is no more. The "what will be" has not yet arrived. Yet this transition zone is not the end of anyone's story. It is a time rich with promise even if it does not seem like that at the moment. The psalmists have sprinkled that hope all through their works.

> Happy are the people whose strength is in you! Whose hearts are set on the pilgrims' way. Those who go through the desolate valley will find it a place of springs, for the early rains have covered it with pools of water. (Ps. 84:4–5, BCP)

> Create in me a clean heart, O God, and renew a right spirit within me. Cast me not away from your presence and take not your holy Spirit from me. Give me the joy of your saving help again and sustain me with your bountiful Spirit. (Ps. 51:11–13, BCP)

We have a choice in finding this new normal. We can look at the journey as a terrible ending of something treasured or we can look at it as a beginning of something new, as hard as that might seem in the moment. Regardless, we are not alone. God was with us on the old familiar path and is with us now on this new path. In time this new direction will not feel so strange and little delights will begin to show their faces, much like snowdrops that surface through the winter's melting snow. Keep watch, therefore; you might find a bit of God's humor along the way:

Oh LORD, how manifold are your works! in wisdom you have made them all; the earth is full of your creatures. Yonder is the great and wide sea with its living things too many to number, creatures both small and great. There move the ships, and there is that Leviathan, which you have made for the sport of it. (Ps. 104:25–27, BCP)

God is never quiet, never still. Mystery weaves its way through the jumble of all that clangs and collides and demands our attention. God does not let us hide away for very long either. When we cry out, there are answers, just not always in the ways we expect. When we give up, we are nourished by the meager strength that is in us. And when our wintered hearts have rested for enough time, God makes manifest the love, compassion, and courage that have been there all along. That light still shines but now with deeper insight of gratitude, understanding, and awareness. Our new path is lovingly strewn with fresh delights that are ours to see and behold. God calls us by name and that name is "beloved."

The words of the psalmists beckon us on year after year, generation upon generation. We are not alone in those disasters that befall us for God is there too.

Your word is a lantern to my feet and a light upon my path. (Ps. 119:105, BCP)

Your love, O LORD, forever will I sing; from age to age my mouth will proclaim your faithfulness. For I am persuaded that your love is established for ever; you have set your faithfulness firmly in the heavens. (Ps. 89:1–2, BCP)

He who dwells in the shelter of the Most High, abides under the shadow of the Almighty. He shall say to the LORD, "You are my refuge and my stronghold, my God in whom I put my trust." . . . For he shall give his angels charge over you, to keep you in all your ways. They shall bear you in their hands, lest you dash your foot against a stone. (Ps. 91:1–2, 11–12, BCP)

I lift up my eyes to the hills; from where is my help to come? My help comes from the LORD, the maker of heaven and earth. He will not let your foot be moved; he who watches over you will not fall asleep. Behold, he who keeps watch over Israel shall neither slumber nor sleep.

The LORD himself watches over you; the LORD is your shade at your right hand. So that the sun shall not strike you by day, nor the moon by night. The LORD shall preserve you from all evil; it is he who shall keep you safe. The LORD shall watch over your going out and your coming in, from this time forth for evermore. (Ps. 121, BCP)

Amen.

Connecting with the Psalms

As suggested in this chapter, take a few verses from various psalms and reach into them emotionally. Read each one several times slowly, pausing where a word or phrase nudges you and speaks to you. Sink into what the author is trying to describe. Open your own emotions into what the author might have been feeling or describing as his own life experience. Walk in the shoes of the author. Is there something present with which your own experience resonates?

Here are some suggested passages that appeared earlier in the chapter to consider:

When I consider your heavens, the work of your fingers, the moon and the stars you have set in their course, what is man that you should be mindful of him? The son of man that you should seek him out? (Ps. 8:4–5, BCP)

LORD, you have searched me out and known me; you know my sitting down and my rising up; you discern my thoughts from afar. . . Where can I go then from your Spirit? where can I flee from your presence? (Ps. 139:1, 6, BCP)

I remember you upon my bed, and meditate on you in the night watches. For you have been my helper, and under the shadow of your wings I will rejoice. (Ps. 63:6–7, BCP)

Pondering

What psalms reside in your personal story? If you were to write a psalm of your story, would it be a lament? A song of thanksgiving? A cry for help? Either as a group or as an individual exercise, pick some piece of your own life story and write a psalm to express the associated emotion.

CHAPTER 17

Where Do You Put the Spaces?

A Story of Discovering God in the Neighborhood

Reflect: Where do you see God
at work in the world?

Read: 1 Samuel 3:1–10

S OME SAY FREUD never sleeps. Is our trickster mind at work all
the time with an agenda of which we are not always aware?
Here is a little experiment to try: look at the text box below
that has twelve letters in it but no space in between. When you look
at it, what do you immediately see?

GODISNOWHERE

If you look at it one way, there is a three-word sentence: "God is
nowhere." If you look at it another way, there is a four-word sentence:
"God is now here."

Where does your mind put the spaces?

That simple question is actually somewhat profound. It is a
metaphor that defines where we will locate ourselves between hope
and despair. If we make the shift of one additional space in the middle
of a jumble of letters where there is no space, we change a message

of grief, disappointment, and loss into one of hope, love, courage, and forgiveness. The creative tension that is generated between those two very different messages is where God frequently does the best work. When one shifts the angle of awareness, God's presence is felt. Is God hidden in plain sight more often than we realize? Consider the story of Eli, a temple priest, and his protégé, Samuel.

Samuel was a young man who had been dedicated to God's service by his mother, Hannah, and he served the LORD as a servant to Eli, the temple priest. These were hard times as the writer points out: "The word of the LORD was rare in those days; visions were not widespread" (1 Sam. 3:1b). I imagine Eli plodding through each day growing older and frailer, doing the routines that were his duty while his own out-of-control priest-sons carried on scandalously. But Samuel's presence was a blessing for Eli, and Samuel grew "both in stature and in favor with the LORD and the people" (1 Sam. 2:26). In this young man, Eli had the opportunity to groom and shape a promising young person who might follow in Eli's footsteps one day. At least he would not die feeling like life, and his own offspring, had been a total disappointment.

One night, while both were sleeping, Samuel heard a voice calling his name, "Samuel. Samuel." The boy jumped up, thinking that it was his master calling him. He woke Eli up, saying, "Here I am, for you called me." Eli responded, "What? Go back to bed. I didn't call you." So Samuel obeyed and went back to bed. The LORD called a second time, "Samuel. Samuel." And a second time Samuel ran into his master's chamber, but his master sent him back, saying, "I did not call you." When this happened a third time, Eli, who was more experienced in these kinds of things, finally had new insight into what was happening. He shifted his thinking about what God might be doing; he instructed Samuel what to say if this should happen yet again. So when God called a fourth time, Samuel did not run to his master, Eli. Instead, as instructed by Eli, he answered, "Speak, LORD. For your servant is listening."

Eli and Samuel had no idea how this would turn out. Neither of them had any way of knowing that Samuel was now on a trajectory that would lead to his becoming one the most important prophets of his day and a key personality in the developing history of the Hebrew people. The shift of perspective that God might well be doing something different shaped the rest of Samuel's life.

"Speak, LORD. For your servant is listening." Perhaps we (including our churches) should be praying that phrase more often ourselves.

Our own internal conversations shape what we want to see rather than allowing us to "tune in" to what God might want us to find.

> When God meets us where we are, we're invited to see our lives and world through different eyes. We see that what once seemed godforsaken is [exactly] where God is present and at work. . . . We come to recognize leadership as less about managing people into the plans, programs, and visions leaders create, and more about accompanying people on the Way of Jesus as we help them reinterpret their lives and world in light of the gospel. . . . We must rehear the stories of imperfect, doubting, unfinished humans like us being entrusted by God with seemingly impossible callings and promises—futures into which they typically stumble rather than achieve with competence and mastery. In, through, and sometimes in spite of their very humanity, God sets about restoring the world. We inhabit the same story today.[48]

Instead of listening, we lament that things are not the same as they used to be. Our energies are spent trying to fix something that possibly should not be "fixed" at all; at least, not in the way we keep trying. Perhaps, instead, we are being invited to adapt and learn from new circumstances.

Can it be that the light of God's love is shining all around us but the Church, distracted by traditions, operational necessities, and various agendas, is a bit too burdened to look at things through new lenses? Are the stories of those outside our church buildings showing us God's hand at work as the living Scripture of our day? Is God beckoning us to stumble into the future, not to arrive with already prepared solutions to a problem, but to watch, listen, imagine, wonder, and learn from what is really taking place outside of our sacred selves? What if we, like Eli, were to shift the spaces in our thinking to discover that "God is now here," only in camouflaged ways?

At twenty-four years old, Veronika Scott found herself the creator and founder of a small business that, stitch by stitch, was making quiet strides in addressing poverty and homelessness in Detroit. While in design school, a class project had to address some need in

---

48 Dwight J. Zscheile, *The Agile Church: Spirit-Led Innovation in an Uncertain Age* (New York: Morehouse Publishing, 2014), 35.

society. She spent time studying homeless shelters and designed a warm coat that, with a few zips, could turn into a sleeping bag. She made prototypes and distributed them to people on the street and homeless shelters in order to get feedback on the coats. She tells of one day when a woman at one shelter yelled at her, "We don't need coats! We need jobs!" Veronika said, "She was right. A coat was just a Band-Aid. They needed to address the systemic issue of unemployment that made people homeless in the first place." She went on to develop The Empowerment Plan,[49] employing only women who have been living in shelters. They are given training in whatever they need to be successful: sewing skills from a professional seamstress, technical preparation, experience, and guidance in business practices. Not only are these unique coats being produced and distributed to the homeless internationally, but these formerly homeless women are now employed and have a means to support their families.

Is this one way in which God's yearning for justice and dignity is alive in Detroit?

As a young twenty-seven-year-old investment banker, Mason Wartman decided to change his career and open a pizza store in his hometown of Philadelphia. Rosa's Fresh Pizza opened in late 2013, selling pizza at a dollar a slice. A few months after opening, a customer asked if he could prepurchase a slice for the next person who came in and was short of money. He described a custom in Italy where customers could prepurchase coffee for people who could not afford one. It was an intriguing idea to consider, so Mason tried it out. He bought stacks of Post-it notes, started telling customers about this new custom at Rosa's Pizza, and word spread quickly. Thus was born the tradition of prepurchasing pizza slices for those who could not afford one. Each prepurchased slice has a Post-it note hung on the wall for anyone to claim a free slice of pizza. Not only have thousands of pizza slices been sold and distributed to the hungry, but words of encouragement written on the Post-it notes by the purchasers offer reassurance, inspiration, and caring from strangers to those who need to find hope as well as food. "Rosa's Fresh Pizza: Helping the Community One Slice at a Time" is described as "an elegant solution" to building a business that will feed stomachs as well as hungry souls.[50]

The Reverend Molly Baskette comments: "It's not charity. It's

---

49 See www.empowermentplan.org and https://youtu.be/mo-kvh1w60w.
50 See https://vimeo.com/154885946.

communion. Charity can do a lot of good, but charity also sometimes brings dented castoffs from the back of the pantry to the food drive and calls it love. Charity makes inequality radically visible. Communion makes inequality radically invisible."[51]

Pizza and Post-it notes—contemporary "outward and visible signs of inward and spiritual grace."[52] Sacraments revealing love in action; God hidden in plain sight in a pizza store.

At four years old, Jaden lost his father. Two years later, his mother died suddenly in her sleep. Now living with his aunt in Savannah, Georgia, he set out on a personal "Smile Experiment" to make people smile, because making them happy helped him feel happier too. Walking through the streets and markets of Savannah with his aunt, he distributed small toys that he had purchased and offered them to anyone who seemed to need a bit of happiness, in order to simply "make people smile."[53] What must it be like to be a surprised recipient of one of Jaden's simple gifts? What power does a small plastic palm tree have when accompanied by the eager gaze of a young child who yearns to simply bring you joy? It is reminiscent of the gifts brought by the Magi to a manger bed so long ago—gifts meant for a king that were carried from afar to honor the newborn for whom they were intended. Jaden's gifts are not gold, frankincense, and myrrh, but they are intended nonetheless to honor the person in front of him. The price doesn't matter. It is the light of uncompromising love that shines through such a gift that gives it a sweeping value. Jaden is transforming his own devastated world and that of other people, one bit of reverence at a time. Is it possible for God to be at work in the compassion of a grieving six-year-old?

The Reverend Matt Fitzgerald writes:

> Years ago I was in a parishioner's kitchen an hour or so after he died. His wife was in the living room with his body. Their teenage daughter, a church friend, and I were at the kitchen table. We tried to speak comfort to one another, but we'd run out of things to say. We sat in silence. To me it felt like we were waiting. But waiting for what? The funeral

---

51 Molly Baskette, "Pay It Forward," *Still Speaking Daily Devotional* (United Church of Christ, April 18, 2015), www.ucc.org/daily_devotional_pay_it_forward.

52 BCP, 857.

53 "Little Boy Collects Smiles in Downtown Savannah After Losing Both Parents," originally broadcast July 23, 2015, www.wtoc.com/story/29621107/little-boy-collects-smiles-in-downtown-savannah-after-losing-both-parents.

home was due to take away the body. That would only make things worse.

Then the doorbell rang and a plumber stepped in. An hour earlier the hospice nurse had followed protocol and flushed all of the dead man's medications down the drain. This broke the toilet. The plumber knew none of this. He just walked into raw grief, a pastor out of words, a reeling family, and the recently deceased right there in the living room. He could have run straight to the bathroom. But he didn't.

He shook my hand, looked the teenage daughter straight in the eyes, and told the grieving widow that he knew what a good man her husband was. As he made his rounds, something in the room turned. For a moment the pain broke and became something else. Or at least the pain was met by a power that promised it would not last forever. Grace comes in the most unlikely guise. Christ comes when we least expect him. "Like a thief in the night." Or a plumber at a deathbed. [54]

Matthew 24:36 shares that no one has any idea when the Son of Man is going to show up. We have no idea what skills the Son of Man will bring either—God showing up in the everyday and partnering with what ordinary people are doing. These stories are holy and sacred in ways that are unexpected, untraditional, and unrestrained. All boundaries drop when compassion is at work.

"It is among ordinary men and women, whose names will not be recorded or remembered, that God shapes a future."[55] Ordinary people responding with compassion to human need, not even realizing they are privy to an extraordinary God hidden in plain sight "whose power working in us does more than we can ask or imagine" (Eph. 3:20b, paraphrase).

These stories matter. They are the bridge that takes us across the chasm just when we think the road has run out. For our churches today, perhaps we are looking in all the wrong places for how to "resurrect" our understanding of mission. It is renewal of the world's spirituality

---

54 The Reverend Matt Fitzgerald, "Like a Plumber," *Still Speaking Daily Devotional* (United Church of Christ, June 6, 2015), www.ucc.org/daily_devotional_like_a_plumber_at_a_deathbed.

55 Alan J. Roxburgh, *Missional: Joining God in the Neighborhood* (Grand Rapids: Baker Books, 2011), 129.

that is moving forward. Traditional institutions are being invited to learn what role is theirs as God continues to lean into the future. Perhaps we are exactly the right people to be watching and wondering what God is up to. Our God has been occupied in surprising ways even before Jesus left the tomb. Our twenty-first-century quandary about survival as a "modern church" should be no exception to the all-encompassing persistence of the Holy One. Perhaps we are the ones to ask the right questions and make sense of the puzzle pieces to create a picture of God's dreams that have been forgotten over time or lost due to our own wandering ways.

> I believe we are being invited to lay aside all our church questions with all their programs designed to answer our questions about how to reach more people. We are to lay aside our anxious need to say the right words at the right place to get the right decisions and we are to enter the households, work beside people, and sit at tables where we can listen to their stories and enter their dialogue and, perhaps, catch the wind of the Spirit as he births new forms of witness and life in a time grown tired of church conversations.[56]

It is precisely at the intersection of our fear and our faith where the unknown future sends messages. It comes from the pizza shop, the factory sewing room, the homeless shelter, the death bed, the plumber's personal toolbox, and the experiment to collect smiles, to remind us that God is alive and well in our world.

We would do well to respond like Samuel: "Speak, LORD. For your servant is listening."

Connecting with Eli

Long ago, you became a priest. Actually, it was always predetermined that you should be a priest. That is the function of your tribe in Israel. You are the caretakers of the holy. But it seems that while the Ark of God was close at hand in the Temple of Shiloh, the presence of God was not. Your sons, who had inherited the priesthood, ran amuck. The priesthood had deteriorated with their abuse of power and privilege and you couldn't do anything to stop them. Day by day you grew older

---

56 Ibid., 145.

and more discouraged. Then Samuel came into your life to be a servant to you. Dedicated to this role of service, he was the hope of the future you had wished your own sons could have been.

Your own dormant skill as an interpreter of God's presence found usefulness the night Samuel kept waking you up. After the third time of having your sleep disturbed, your underlying inner knowledge about the mysterious ways of God emerged. You realized you held the key that Samuel would need in order to hear God's message. Nothing in the temple changed, but your perspective shifted, allowing God to be present to Samuel in a way that would shape the rest of his young life and yours. What was it like to play such a key role after such a long time of tending a dying and disenchanted priesthood? Were you curious or disappointed that God did not seem to want to talk directly to you?

Pondering

GODISNOWHERE. What did you first "see" when you looked at these letters strung together: "God is nowhere" or "God is now here"? What does that suggest to you? Is your glass half full or half empty?

The Empowerment Plan, Rosa's Pizza, Jaden's Smile Experiment, and the plumber at the deathbed took place outside of the involvement of the formal Church. Is that God's hand at work? What do these things have to teach the Church about the ways in which God is moving the Church?

The Light Shines Through

Transforming the Gloom

Reflect: Where has God been at
work in your own story?

Read: Isaiah 55:6–11

THIS IS A holy place. It is quiet and peace-filled here in the predawn hours. I don't often come to this historic sanctuary of Trinity Episcopal Church so early in the morning, but this week is different. It is Holy Week and today dawns as Good Friday, the day Jesus will yet again die on the cross.

Holy Week spiritually engages us with the divine and dreadful mystery of betrayal, death, and the finality of Good Friday. Much like the original day after Jesus was arrested, the daily routines and looming to-do lists are just now coming to life as the day begins here in Shelburne, Vermont. Yet the yearning of the Spirit gently declares its attendance in this quiet envelope of safety. I am torn between remaining here feeling God's presence or turning my face toward the day and the tasks out in front of me. There is time for that, I suppose. For now there is only sanctuary. Peace. Presence.

It is the smell of old wood, old books, furniture polish, and the haunting drift of incense that suggests the ways in which this house of prayer has been touched by the legacies of loving hands. It is a storehouse of pleas yearned into the silence. It is a kind vessel for tears wept in the depths of despair. Its vaulted ceiling has soaked up the shimmer of song lifted into space. The invisible patina of reverence ages this place gracefully as layer upon layer, generation upon generation, come and go, leaving the mark of memory in their wake.

All this is present in the dark silence as a daily ritual is about to begin. The pride of this congregation is about to take center stage as the three tall windows of colored glass created by the genius of the great Louis Comfort Tiffany—the unmatched stained glass artist of his day—prepare themselves yet again to receive the gift that will cause their beauty to blaze. It doesn't matter if there is no one here to see it except me. The show would go on regardless. Beauty is as beauty does. The gift of light transforms the gloom whenever it throws its command against the darkness, whether anyone bears witness or not.

The initial band of sunlight draws slowly and silently across the first darkened pane as the sun continues its leisurely ascent. Ever so slowly—one by one—the brilliant fragments proclaim their alleluia to the day and shatter the solemn grayness with color as the images of Jesus, flanked by John the Baptist and John the Evangelist, take up their daily vigil yet again today.

The subjects and stories represented in glass are frozen in time and yet there is an element missing. Regardless of the artistic skill of their creator, the quality of materials, and the subject matter represented, there is only one component that makes these windows so magnificent—only one thing that unlocks their story. The light.

It is the soundless and persistent light steadfastly shining through them that unlocks their beautiful fire and turns them from expensive pieces of colored glass into an encounter with the Holy. All without a single inspirational word spoken or a single note sung, just the light shining through them. These priceless windows were made to be pathways for the light.

It is not a far stretch, then, to consider that we, too, are like these masterpieces of artistry. We are each a deeply unique design. Our lives have been etched by different experiences. And, like a stained glass work of art in a sacred sanctuary, it is God's light shining through us that makes visible the invisible and unlocks the brilliant mystery that dwells within each of us. We, too, were made to be instruments for the light—God's light.

While stained glass windows themselves are stationary, the

stories represented within them certainly are not. They are sacred snapshots of various individuals who really existed on this planet at one point in time and are reminders that someone's unique story was really God disclosing something new to us as well.

Imagine our own life stories as a series of vignettes making up multiple panes of a stained glass window. What mini-story would each pane of glass depict? What are the inspired moments that shine with delight? What are the shameful yet teachable moments that would sooner be forgotten? What insights, encounters, and experiences of our lives link us with those whose iconic stories are presented in Scripture?

Are there places where we are crouched away under our own proverbial broom tree, exhausted by life circumstances and in need of God's care and tending like Elijah? Are we Joseph going along in the normalcy of our day but suddenly finding ourselves between a rock and a hard place with God inconveniently hidden in plain sight in the midst of it? Are we Peter with an expectation that we must "follow the rules" but instead getting surprised by God moving in an unexpected direction and wanting us to go there too? Are we the man blind from birth who, simply by being healed, unintentionally challenges the status quo? Sometimes the greatest moments for witness are plunked unknowingly in our laps. Are we Mary Magdalene lost in grief without any way of knowing that joy follows in the morning? Are we Jairus, the town official, throwing himself in despair upon God's mercy in order to save a beloved child who is in danger? Are we Judas, whose ambition drove him to trust in himself more than in the startling compassion of a forgiving God?

These stories are all distinctive. The times and cultures represented are all different. Choices made and steps taken into the unknown are all diverse, but the one common element is that God's light and love shone through and provided what was needed in the moment. Like the ancients, we might not know how our stories will turn out, but that doesn't stop God from moving with finesse and artistry through our day-to-day existence, accomplishing whatever it is God has in mind at any given time. We are the windows through which God touches the world and in that sense, our stories *are* God's story.

Is God lurking closer than you realize? What underlying glimmer of hope and courage is slumbering in your story and waiting to be born in new ways? What light is already shining that might be hard to perceive at times? These are resurrection moments that might catch us unawares and in unforeseen ways, but catch us they do.

> The resurrection is a description of how the universe self-corrects, life always reasserting itself even when forces of death and darkness have temporarily prevailed. Like a tiny flower growing through cracks in broken cement, peace of mind emerging at last after periods of deep grief, or people continuing to fall in love despite the ravages of war, love always gets the final say. To lean on the resurrection is simply to recognize what's true: if happiness hasn't arrived yet, then the story isn't over. Easter isn't the story of something that happened to only man [*sic*] over two thousand years ago; it's the revelation of God's eternal imprint on every moment, for every life. It is the potential for light that exists within even the deepest darkness. It is the reason to hope when all hope seems lost. It is the possibility for a new beginning that seems impossible when all has gone wrong. . . . Our openness to infinite possibility—a willingness to consider that there might be another way—is the mind of man allowing itself to be illuminated by God.[57]

We have reached the end of these stories for now. It is my hope that at least one or two new insights might have come your way if you have reached this point on the page. God's story is never still, never quiet, never finished. It has run true since the beginning of time, always carving deeper into the souls of humankind like an ancient river cutting a deep canyon. The women and men, ancient and modern, whose stories we share are fellow travelers on a soul journey with a Creator Being that we might not always understand. But God knows our stories with all their warts and wobbles and loves us still, regardless of the parts we might not love so much. Our task is to "trust in the slow work of God,"[58] for God will ultimately get what God wants.

---

57 Marianne Williamson, "The Alchemy of Easter," April 5, 2015, https://www.facebook.com/williamsonmarianne/posts/10155350755215580.

58 Pierre Teilhard de Chardin, "Patient Trust," in *Hearts on Fire: Praying with the Jesuits*, ed. Michael Harter (Chicago: Loyola Press, 2005), 107.

Connecting with Yourself

Draw your own stained glass window. Create either one big window representative of something significant in your life or a window made up of many windowpanes, each one depicting some significant life event that has shaped your own spiritual journey. (*Materials needed: large drawing paper, markers, pencils, crayons, ruler.*)

Pondering

Reflect on your drawing. Where was God's light shining through those pieces of your story? Did you realize it at the time? How do you understand your personal story as part of God's ongoing story?

How does it feel to realize that you don't know how your story will turn out? What resonance do you find, if any, with stories in Scripture where the people didn't know how their stories would turn out?

Where has God been at work in your story? Have there been times when God's presence has seemed distant or nonexistent? Have there been times when God's presence has been very near? What has it been like to experience either of those times?

Scripture Stories

Chapter 1: A Story of God's Covenant with Abraham

Genesis 15:1–16

After these things the word of the LORD came to Abram in a vision, "Do not be afraid, Abram, I am your shield; your reward shall be very great." But Abram said, "O Lord GOD, what will you give me, for I continue childless, and the heir of my house is Eliezer of Damascus?" And Abram said, "You have given me no offspring, and so a slave born in my house is to be my heir." But the word of the LORD came to him, "This man shall not be your heir; no one but your very own issue shall be your heir." He brought him outside and said, "Look toward heaven and count the stars, if you are able to count them." Then he said to him, "So shall your descendants be." And he believed the LORD; and the LORD reckoned it to him as righteousness.

Genesis 17:1–7

When Abram was ninety-nine years old, the LORD appeared to Abram, and said to him, "I am God Almighty; walk before me, and be blameless. And I will make my covenant between me and you, and will make you exceedingly numerous." Then Abram fell on his face; and God said to him, "As for me, this is my covenant with you: You shall be the ancestor of a multitude of nations. No longer shall your name be Abram, but your name shall be Abraham; for I have made you the ancestor of a multitude of nations. I will make you exceedingly fruitful; and I will make nations of you, and kings shall come from you. I will establish my covenant between me and you, and your offspring after you throughout their generations, for an everlasting covenant, to be God to you and to your offspring after you."

Chapter 2: A Story of Jesus and Peter

Matthew 16:13–24

Now when Jesus came into the district of Caesarea Philippi, he asked his disciples, "Who do people say that the Son of Man is?" And they said, "Some say John the Baptist, but others Elijah, and still others Jeremiah or one of the prophets." He said to them, "But who do you say that I am?" Simon Peter answered, "You are the Messiah, the Son of the living God." And Jesus answered him, "Blessed are you, Simon son of Jonah! For flesh and blood has not revealed this to you, but my Father in heaven. And I tell you, you are Peter, and on this rock I will build my church, and the gates of Hades will not prevail against it. I will give you the keys of the kingdom of heaven, and whatever you bind on earth will be bound in heaven, and whatever you loose on earth will be loosed in heaven." Then he sternly ordered the disciples not to tell anyone that he was the Messiah.

From that time on, Jesus began to show his disciples that he must go to Jerusalem and undergo great suffering at the hands of the elders and chief priests and scribes, and be killed, and on the third day be raised. And Peter took him aside and began to rebuke him, saying, "God forbid it, Lord! This must never happen to you." But he turned and said to Peter, "Get behind me, Satan! You are a stumbling block to me; for you are setting your mind not on divine things but on human things."

Then Jesus told his disciples, "If any want to become my followers, let them deny themselves and take up their cross and follow me."

Chapter 3: A Story of Nicodemus

John 3:1–10
Now there was a Pharisee named Nicodemus, a leader of the Jews. He came to Jesus by night and said to him, "Rabbi, we know that you are a teacher who has come from God; for no one can do these signs that you do apart from the presence of God." Jesus answered him, "Very truly, I tell you, no one can see the kingdom of God without being born from above." Nicodemus said to him, "How can anyone be born after having grown old? Can one enter a second time into the mother's womb and be born?" Jesus answered, "Very truly, I tell you, no one can enter the kingdom of God without being born of water and Spirit. What is born of the flesh is flesh, and what is born of the Spirit is spirit. Do not be astonished that I said to you, 'You must be born from above.' The wind blows where it chooses, and you hear the sound of it, but you do not know where it comes from or where it goes. So it is with everyone who is born of the Spirit." Nicodemus said to him, "How can these things be?" Jesus answered him, "Are you a teacher of Israel, and yet you do not understand these things?

John 7:45–52
Then the temple police went back to the chief priests and Pharisees, who asked them, "Why did you not arrest him?" The police answered, "Never has anyone spoken like this!" Then the Pharisees replied, "Surely you have not been deceived too, have you? Has any one of the authorities or of the Pharisees believed in him? But this crowd, which does not know the law— they are accursed." Nicodemus, who had gone to Jesus before, and who was one of them, asked, "Our law does not judge people without first giving

them a hearing to find out what they are doing, does it?" They replied, "Surely you are not also from Galilee, are you? Search and you will see that no prophet is to arise from Galilee."

John 19:38–42

After these things, Joseph of Arimathea, who was a disciple of Jesus, though a secret one because of his fear of the Jews, asked Pilate to let him take away the body of Jesus. Pilate gave him permission; so he came and removed his body. Nicodemus, who had at first come to Jesus by night, also came, bringing a mixture of myrrh and aloes, weighing about a hundred pounds. They took the body of Jesus and wrapped it with the spices in linen cloths, according to the burial custom of the Jews. Now there was a garden in the place where he was crucified, and in the garden there was a new tomb in which no one had ever been laid. And so, because it was the Jewish day of Preparation, and the tomb was nearby, they laid Jesus there.

Chapter 4: A Story of Jairus and a Story of the Hemorrhaging Woman

Mark 5:21–42

When Jesus had crossed again in the boat to the other side, a great crowd gathered around him; and he was by the lake. Then one of the leaders of the synagogue named Jairus came and, when he saw him, fell at his feet and begged him repeatedly, "My little daughter is at the point of death. Come and lay your hands on her, so that she may be made well, and live." So he went with him.

And a large crowd followed him and pressed in on him. Now there was a woman who had been suffering from hemorrhages for twelve years. She had endured much under many physicians, and had spent all that she had; and she was no better, but rather grew worse. She had heard about Jesus, and came up behind him in the crowd and touched his cloak, for she said, "If I but touch his clothes, I will be made well." Immediately her hemorrhage stopped; and she felt in her body that she was healed of her disease. Immediately aware that power had gone forth from him, Jesus turned about in the crowd and said, "Who touched my clothes?" And his disciples said to him, "You see the crowd pressing in on you; how can you say, 'Who touched me?'" He looked all around to see who had done it. But the woman, knowing what had happened to her, came in fear and trembling, fell down before him, and told him the whole truth. He said to her, "Daughter, your faith has made you well; go in peace, and be healed of your disease."

While he was still speaking, some people came from the leader's house to say, "Your daughter is dead. Why trouble the teacher any further?" But overhearing what they said, Jesus said to the leader of the synagogue, "Do not fear, only believe." He allowed no one to follow him except Peter, James, and John, the brother of James. When they came to the house of the leader of the synagogue, he saw a commotion, people weeping and wailing loudly. When he had entered, he said to them, "Why do you make a commotion and weep? The child is not dead but sleeping." And they laughed at him. Then he put them all outside, and took the child's father and mother and those who were with him, and went in where the child was. He took her by the hand and said to her, "Talitha cum," which means, "Little girl, get up!" And immediately the girl got up and began to walk about (she was twelve years of age). At this they were overcome with amazement.

Chapter 5: A Story of Elijah

1 Kings 19:4–8
But he himself went a day's journey into the wilderness, and came and sat down under a solitary broom tree. He asked that he might die: "It is enough; now, O LORD, take away my life, for I am no better than my ancestors." Then he lay down under the broom tree and fell asleep. Suddenly an angel touched him and said to him, "Get up and eat." He looked, and there at his head was a cake baked on hot stones, and a jar of water. He ate and drank, and lay down again. The angel of the LORD came a second time, touched him, and said, "Get up and eat, otherwise the journey will be too much for you." He got up, and ate and drank; then he went in the strength of that food forty days and forty nights to Horeb the mount of God.

Chapter 6: A Story of Aaron and the Golden Calf

Exodus 32:1–6
When the people saw that Moses delayed to come down from the mountain, the people gathered around Aaron, and said to him, "Come, make gods for us, who shall go before us; as for this Moses, the man who brought us up out of the land of Egypt, we do not know what has become of him." Aaron said to them, "Take off the gold rings that are on the ears of your wives, your sons, and your daughters, and bring them to me." So all the people took off the gold rings from their ears, and brought them to Aaron. He took the gold from them, formed it in a mold, and cast an image of a calf; and they said, "These are your gods, O Israel, who brought you up out of the land of Egypt!" When Aaron saw this, he built an altar before it; and Aaron made proclamation and said, "Tomorrow shall be a festival to the LORD." They rose early the next day, and offered burnt offerings and brought sacrifices of well-being; and the people sat down to eat and drink, and rose up to revel.

Chapter 7: A Story of the Good Shepherd

Psalm 23

The LORD is my shepherd;
  I shall not be in want.
He makes me lie down in green pastures
  and leads me beside still waters.
He revives my soul
  and guides me along right pathways for his Name's sake.
Though I walk through the valley of the shadow of death,
I shall fear no evil;
  for you are with me;
  your rod and your staff, they comfort me.
You spread a table before me in the presence of those
  who trouble me;
  you have anointed my head with oil,
  and my cup is running over.
Surely your goodness and mercy shall follow me all the days
  of my life,
  and I will dwell in the house of the LORD for ever.

Chapter 8: A Story of Mary Magdalene at the Tomb

John 20:1–18

Early on the first day of the week, while it was still dark, Mary Magdalene came to the tomb and saw that the stone had been removed from the tomb. So she ran and went to Simon Peter and the other disciple, the one whom Jesus loved, and said to them, "They have taken the Lord out of the tomb, and we do not know where they have laid him." Then Peter and the other disciple set out and went towards the tomb. The two were running together, but the other disciple outran Peter and reached the tomb first. He bent down to look in and saw the linen wrappings lying there, but he did not go in. Then Simon Peter came, following him, and went into the tomb. He saw the linen wrappings lying there, and the cloth that had been on Jesus' head, not lying with the linen wrappings but rolled up in a place by itself. Then the other disciple, who reached the tomb first, also went in, and he saw and believed; for as yet they did not understand the scripture, that he must rise from the dead. Then the disciples returned to their homes.

But Mary stood weeping outside the tomb. As she wept, she bent over to look into the tomb; and she saw two angels in white, sitting where the body of Jesus had been lying, one at the head and the other at the feet. They said to her, "Woman, why are you weeping?" She said to them, "They have taken away my LORD, and I do not know where they have laid him."

When she had said this, she turned around and saw Jesus standing there, but she did not know that it was Jesus. Jesus said to her, "Woman, why are you weeping? Whom are you looking for?" Supposing him to be the gardener, she said to him, "Sir, if you have carried him away, tell me where you have laid him, and I will take him away." Jesus said to her, "Mary!" She turned and said to him in Hebrew, "Rabbouni!" (which means Teacher). Jesus said to her, "Do not hold on to me, because I have not yet ascended to the Father. But go to my brothers and say to them, 'I am ascending to my Father and your Father, to my God and your God.'" Mary Magdalene went and announced to the disciples, "I have seen the Lord"; and she told them that he had said these things to her.

Chapter 9: A Story of Judas Iscariot

Matthew 26:14–16
Then one of the twelve, who was called Judas Iscariot, went to the chief priests and said, "What will you give me if I betray him to you?" They paid him thirty pieces of silver. And from that moment he began to look for an opportunity to betray him.

Matthew 26:47–50
While he was still speaking, Judas, one of the twelve, arrived; with him was a large crowd with swords and clubs, from the chief priests and the elders of the people. Now the betrayer had given them a sign, saying, "The one I will kiss is the man; arrest him." At once he came up to Jesus and said, "Greetings, Rabbi!" and kissed him. Jesus said to him, "Friend, do what you are here to do." Then they came and laid hands on Jesus and arrested him.

Chapter 10: A Story of the Disciples on the Road to Emmaus

Luke 24:13–35
Now on that same day two of them were going to a village called Emmaus, about seven miles from Jerusalem, and talking with each other about all these things that had happened. While they were talking and discussing, Jesus himself came near and went with them, but their eyes were kept from recognizing him. And he said to them, "What are you discussing with each other while you walk along?" They stood still, looking sad. Then one of them, whose name was Cleopas, answered him, "Are you the only stranger in Jerusalem who does not know the things that have taken place there in these days?" He asked them, "What things?" They replied, "The things about Jesus of Nazareth, who was a prophet mighty in deed and word before God

and all the people, and how our chief priests and leaders handed him over to be condemned to death and crucified him. But we had hoped that he was the one to redeem Israel. Yes, and besides all this, it is now the third day since these things took place. Moreover, some women of our group astounded us. They were at the tomb early this morning, and when they did not find his body there, they came back and told us that they had indeed seen a vision of angels who said that he was alive. Some of those who were with us went to the tomb and found it just as the women had said; but they did not see him." Then he said to them, "Oh, how foolish you are, and how slow of heart to believe all that the prophets have declared! Was it not necessary that the Messiah should suffer these things and then enter into his glory?" Then beginning with Moses and all the prophets, he interpreted to them the things about himself in all the scriptures.

As they came near the village to which they were going, he walked ahead as if he were going on. But they urged him strongly, saying, "Stay with us, because it is almost evening and the day is now nearly over." So he went in to stay with them. When he was at the table with them, he took bread, blessed and broke it, and gave it to them. Then their eyes were opened, and they recognized him; and he vanished from their sight. They said to each other, "Were not our hearts burning within us while he was talking to us on the road, while he was opening the scriptures to us?" That same hour they got up and returned to Jerusalem; and they found the eleven and their companions gathered together. They were saying, "The LORD has risen indeed, and he has appeared to Simon!" Then they told what had happened on the road, and how he had been made known to them in the breaking of the bread.

Chapter 11: A Story of Carole

Psalm 139:1–13

> LORD, you have searched me out and known me;
>> you know my sitting down and my rising up;
>> you discern my thoughts from afar.
> You trace my journeys and my resting-places
>> and are acquainted with all my ways.
> Indeed, there is not a word on my lips,
>> but you, O LORD, know it altogether.
> You press upon me behind and before
>> and lay your hand upon me.
> Such knowledge is too wonderful for me;
>> it is so high that I cannot attain to it.
> Where can I go then from your Spirit?
>> where can I flee from your presence?

If I climb up to heaven, you are there;
 if I make the grave my bed, you are there also.
If I take the wings of the morning
 and dwell in the uttermost parts of the sea,
Even there your hand will lead me
 and your right hand hold me fast.
If I say, "Surely the darkness will cover me,
 and the light around me turn to night,"
Darkness is not dark to you;
the night is as bright as the day;
 darkness and light to you are both alike.
For you yourself created my inmost parts;
 you knit me together in my mother's womb.
I will thank you because I am marvelously made;
 your works are wonderful, and I know it well.

Chapter 12: A Story of Peter and Cornelius

Acts 10:1–11:18

In Caesarea there was a man named Cornelius, a centurion of the Italian Cohort, as it was called. He was a devout man who feared God with all his household; he gave alms generously to the people and prayed constantly to God. One afternoon at about three o'clock he had a vision in which he clearly saw an angel of God coming in and saying to him, "Cornelius." He stared at him in terror and said, "What is it, Lord?" He answered, "Your prayers and your alms have ascended as a memorial before God. Now send men to Joppa for a certain Simon who is called Peter; he is lodging with Simon, a tanner, whose house is by the seaside." When the angel who spoke to him had left, he called two of his slaves and a devout soldier from the ranks of those who served him, and after telling them everything, he sent them to Joppa.

About noon the next day, as they were on their journey and approaching the city, Peter went up on the roof to pray. He became hungry and wanted something to eat; and while it was being prepared, he fell into a trance. He saw the heaven opened and something like a large sheet coming down, being lowered to the ground by its four corners. In it were all kinds of four-footed creatures and reptiles and birds of the air. Then he heard a voice saying, "Get up, Peter; kill and eat." But Peter said, "By no means, Lord; for I have never eaten anything that is profane or unclean." The voice said to him again, a second time, "What God has made clean, you must not call profane." This happened three times, and the thing was suddenly taken up to heaven.

Now while Peter was greatly puzzled about what to make of the vision that he had seen, suddenly the men sent by Cornelius appeared. They were asking for Simon's house and were standing by the gate. They called out to ask whether Simon, who was called Peter, was staying there. While Peter was still thinking about the vision, the Spirit said to him, "Look, three men are searching for you. Now get up, go down, and go with them without hesitation; for I have sent them." So Peter went down to the men and said, "I am the one you are looking for; what is the reason for your coming?" They answered, "Cornelius, a centurion, an upright and God-fearing man, who is well spoken of by the whole Jewish nation, was directed by a holy angel to send for you to come to his house and to hear what you have to say." So Peter invited them in and gave them lodging.

The next day he got up and went with them, and some of the believers from Joppa accompanied him. The following day they came to Caesarea. Cornelius was expecting them and had called together his relatives and close friends. On Peter's arrival Cornelius met him, and falling at his feet, worshiped him. But Peter made him get up, saying, "Stand up; I am only a mortal." And as he talked with him, he went in and found that many had assembled; and he said to them, "You yourselves know that it is unlawful for a Jew to associate with or to visit a Gentile; but God has shown me that I should not call anyone profane or unclean. So when I was sent for, I came without objection. Now may I ask why you sent for me?"

Cornelius replied, "Four days ago at this very hour, at three o'clock, I was praying in my house when suddenly a man in dazzling clothes stood before me. He said, 'Cornelius, your prayer has been heard and your alms have been remembered before God. Send therefore to Joppa and ask for Simon, who is called Peter; he is staying in the home of Simon, a tanner, by the sea.' Therefore I sent for you immediately, and you have been kind enough to come. So now all of us are here in the presence of God to listen to all that the LORD has commanded you to say."

Then Peter began to speak to them: "I truly understand that God shows no partiality, but in every nation anyone who fears him and does what is right is acceptable to him. You know the message he sent to the people of Israel, preaching peace by Jesus Christ—he is LORD of all. That message spread throughout Judea, beginning in Galilee after the baptism that John announced: how God anointed Jesus of Nazareth with the Holy Spirit and with power; how he went about doing good and healing all who were oppressed by the devil, for God was with him. We are witnesses to all that he did both in Judea and in Jerusalem. They put him to death by hanging him on a tree; but God raised him on the third day and allowed him to appear, not to all the people but to us who were chosen by God as witnesses, and who ate and drank with him after he rose from the dead. He commanded us to preach to the people and to testify that he is the one ordained by God as judge of the living and the dead. All the prophets testify about him that everyone who believes in him receives forgiveness of sins through his name."

While Peter was still speaking, the Holy Spirit fell upon all who heard the word. The circumcised believers who had come with Peter were astounded that the gift of the Holy Spirit had been poured out even on the Gentiles, for they heard them speaking in tongues and extolling God. Then Peter said, "Can anyone withhold the water for baptizing these people who have received the Holy Spirit just as we have?" So he ordered them to be baptized in the name of Jesus Christ. Then they invited him to stay for several days.

Now the apostles and the believers who were in Judea heard that the Gentiles had also accepted the word of God. So when Peter went up to Jerusalem, the circumcised believers criticized him, saying, "Why did you go to uncircumcised men and eat with them?" Then Peter began to explain it to them, step by step, saying, "I was in the city of Joppa praying, and in a trance I saw a vision. There was something like a large sheet coming down from heaven, being lowered by its four corners; and it came close to me. As I looked at it closely I saw four-footed animals, beasts of prey, reptiles, and birds of the air. I also heard a voice saying to me, 'Get up, Peter; kill and eat.' But I replied, 'By no means, LORD; for nothing profane or unclean has ever entered my mouth.' But a second time the voice answered from heaven, 'What God has made clean, you must not call profane.' This happened three times; then everything was pulled up again to heaven. At that very moment three men, sent to me from Caesarea, arrived at the house where we were. The Spirit told me to go with them and not to make a distinction between them and us. These six brothers also accompanied me, and we entered the man's house. He told us how he had seen the angel standing in his house and saying, 'Send to Joppa and bring Simon, who is called Peter; he will give you a message by which you and your entire household will be saved.' And as I began to speak, the Holy Spirit fell upon them just as it had upon us at the beginning. And I remembered the word of the LORD, how he had said, 'John baptized with water, but you will be baptized with the Holy Spirit.' If then God gave them the same gift that he gave us when we believed in the LORD Jesus Christ, who was I that I could hinder God?" When they heard this, they were silenced. And they praised God, saying, "Then God has given even to the Gentiles the repentance that leads to life."

Chapter 13: A Story of Joseph, Jesus's Stepdad

Matthew 1:18–25
Now the birth of Jesus the Messiah took place in this way. When his mother Mary had been engaged to Joseph, but before they lived together, she was found to be with child from the Holy Spirit. Her husband Joseph, being a

righteous man and unwilling to expose her to public disgrace, planned to dismiss her quietly. But just when he had resolved to do this, an angel of the LORD appeared to him in a dream and said, "Joseph, son of David, do not be afraid to take Mary as your wife, for the child conceived in her is from the Holy Spirit. She will bear a son, and you are to name him Jesus, for he will save his people from their sins." All this took place to fulfill what had been spoken by the LORD through the prophet: "Look, the virgin shall conceive and bear a son, and they shall name him Emmanuel," which means, "God is with us." When Joseph awoke from sleep, he did as the angel of the LORD commanded him; he took her as his wife, but had no marital relations with her until she had borne a son; and he named him Jesus.

Chapter 14: A Story of Peter, Paul, and Alyssa

John 21:1–17

After these things Jesus showed himself again to the disciples by the Sea of Tiberias; and he showed himself in this way. Gathered there together were Simon Peter, Thomas called the Twin, Nathanael of Cana in Galilee, the sons of Zebedee, and two others of his disciples. Simon Peter said to them, "I am going fishing." They said to him, "We will go with you." They went out and got into the boat, but that night they caught nothing.

Just after daybreak, Jesus stood on the beach; but the disciples did not know that it was Jesus. Jesus said to them, "Children, you have no fish, have you?" They answered him, "No." He said to them, "Cast the net to the right side of the boat, and you will find some." So they cast it, and now they were not able to haul it in because there were so many fish. That disciple whom Jesus loved said to Peter, "It is the LORD!" When Simon Peter heard that it was the LORD, he put on some clothes, for he was naked, and jumped into the sea. But the other disciples came in the boat, dragging the net full of fish, for they were not far from the land, only about a hundred yards off.

When they had gone ashore, they saw a charcoal fire there, with fish on it, and bread. Jesus said to them, "Bring some of the fish that you have just caught." So Simon Peter went aboard and hauled the net ashore, full of large fish, a hundred fifty-three of them; and though there were so many, the net was not torn. Jesus said to them, "Come and have breakfast." Now none of the disciples dared to ask him, "Who are you?" because they knew it was the LORD. Jesus came and took the bread and gave it to them, and did the same with the fish. This was now the third time that Jesus appeared to the disciples after he was raised from the dead.

When they had finished breakfast, Jesus said to Simon Peter, "Simon son of John, do you love me more than these?" He said to him, "Yes, LORD; you know that I love you." Jesus said to him, "Feed my lambs." A second time he said to him, "Simon son of John, do you love me?" He said to him,

"Yes, LORD; you know that I love you." Jesus said to him, "Tend my sheep." He said to him the third time, "Simon son of John, do you love me?" Peter felt hurt because he said to him the third time, "Do you love me?" And he said to him, "LORD, you know everything; you know that I love you." Jesus said to him, "Feed my sheep."

Acts 9:1–20

Meanwhile Saul, still breathing threats and murder against the disciples of the LORD, went to the high priest and asked him for letters to the synagogues at Damascus, so that if he found any who belonged to the Way, men or women, he might bring them bound to Jerusalem. Now as he was going along and approaching Damascus, suddenly a light from heaven flashed around him. He fell to the ground and heard a voice saying to him, "Saul, Saul, why do you persecute me?" He asked, "Who are you, LORD?" The reply came, "I am Jesus, whom you are persecuting. But get up and enter the city, and you will be told what you are to do." The men who were traveling with him stood speechless because they heard the voice but saw no one. Saul got up from the ground, and though his eyes were open, he could see nothing; so they led him by the hand and brought him into Damascus. For three days he was without sight, and neither ate nor drank.

Now there was a disciple in Damascus named Ananias. The LORD said to him in a vision, "Ananias." He answered, "Here I am, LORD." The LORD said to him, "Get up and go to the street called Straight, and at the house of Judas look for a man of Tarsus named Saul. At this moment he is praying, and he has seen in a vision a man named Ananias come in and lay his hands on him so that he might regain his sight." But Ananias answered, "LORD, I have heard from many about this man, how much evil he has done to your saints in Jerusalem; and here he has authority from the chief priests to bind all who invoke your name." But the LORD said to him, "Go, for he is an instrument whom I have chosen to bring my name before Gentiles and kings and before the people of Israel; I myself will show him how much he must suffer for the sake of my name." So Ananias went and entered the house. He laid his hands on Saul and said, "Brother Saul, the LORD Jesus, who appeared to you on your way here, has sent me so that you may regain your sight and be filled with the Holy Spirit." And immediately something like scales fell from his eyes, and his sight was restored. Then he got up and was baptized, and after taking some food, he regained his strength. For several days he was with the disciples in Damascus, and immediately he began to proclaim Jesus in the synagogues, saying, "He is the Son of God."

Chapter 15: A Story of the Man Blind from Birth

John 9:1–38

As he walked along, he saw a man blind from birth. His disciples asked him, "Rabbi, who sinned, this man or his parents, that he was born blind?" Jesus answered, "Neither this man nor his parents sinned; he was born blind so that God's works might be revealed in him. We must work the works of him who sent me while it is day; night is coming when no one can work. As long as I am in the world, I am the light of the world." When he had said this, he spat on the ground and made mud with the saliva and spread the mud on the man's eyes, saying to him, "Go, wash in the pool of Siloam" (which means Sent). Then he went and washed and came back able to see.

The neighbors and those who had seen him before as a beggar began to ask, "Is this not the man who used to sit and beg?" Some were saying, "It is he." Others were saying, "No, but it is someone like him." He kept saying, "I am the man." But they kept asking him, "Then how were your eyes opened?" He answered, "The man called Jesus made mud, spread it on my eyes, and said to me, 'Go to Siloam and wash.' Then I went and washed and received my sight." They said to him, "Where is he?" He said, "I do not know."

They brought to the Pharisees the man who had formerly been blind. Now it was a sabbath day when Jesus made the mud and opened his eyes. Then the Pharisees also began to ask him how he had received his sight. He said to them, "He put mud on my eyes. Then I washed, and now I see." Some of the Pharisees said, "This man is not from God, for he does not observe the sabbath." But others said, "How can a man who is a sinner perform such signs?" And they were divided. So they said again to the blind man, "What do you say about him? It was your eyes he opened." He said, "He is a prophet."

The Jews did not believe that he had been blind and had received his sight until they called the parents of the man who had received his sight and asked them, "Is this your son, who you say was born blind? How then does he now see?" His parents answered, "We know that this is our son, and that he was born blind; but we do not know how it is that now he sees, nor do we know who opened his eyes. Ask him; he is of age. He will speak for himself." His parents said this because they were afraid of the Jews; for the Jews had already agreed that anyone who confessed Jesus to be the Messiah would be put out of the synagogue. Therefore his parents said, "He is of age; ask him."

So for the second time they called the man who had been blind, and they said to him, "Give glory to God! We know that this man is a sinner." He answered, "I do not know whether he is a sinner. One thing I do know, that though I was blind, now I see." They said to him, "What did he do to you? How did he open your eyes?" He answered them, "I have told you already, and you would not listen. Why do you want to hear it again? Do you also want to become his disciples?" Then they reviled him, saying, "You are his disciple, but we are disciples of Moses. We know that God has spoken to Moses, but as for this man, we do not know where he comes from." The man answered, "Here is an astonishing thing! You do not know where he comes from, and yet he opened my eyes. We know that God does not listen to sinners, but he does listen to one who worships him and obeys his will. Never since the world began has it been heard that anyone opened the eyes of a person born blind. If this man were not from God, he could do nothing." They answered him, "You were born entirely in sins, and are you trying to teach us?" And they drove him out.

Jesus heard that they had driven him out, and when he found him, he said, "Do you believe in the Son of Man?" He answered, "And who is he, sir? Tell me, so that I may believe in him." Jesus said to him, "You have seen him, and the one speaking with you is he." He said, "Lord, I believe." And he worshiped him.

Chapter 16: A Story of Despair—A Story of Healing

Psalm 40:1–14
> I waited patiently upon the LORD;
>> he stooped to me and heard my cry.
> He lifted me out of the desolate pit, out of the mire and clay;
>> he set my feet upon a high cliff and made my footing sure.
> He put a new song in my mouth,
> a song of praise to our God;
>> many shall see, and stand in awe,
>> and put their trust in the LORD.
> Happy are they who trust in the LORD!
>> they do not resort to evil spirits or turn to false gods.
> Great things are they that you have done, O LORD my God!
> how great your wonders and your plans for us!
>> there is none who can be compared with you.
> Oh, that I could make them known and tell them!
>> but they are more than I can count.
> In sacrifice and offering you take no pleasure
>> (you have given me ears to hear you);
> Burnt-offering and sin-offering you have not required,
>> and so I said, "Behold, I come.
> In the roll of the book it is written concerning me:
>> 'I love to do your will, O my God;
>> you law is deep in my heart.'"

I proclaimed righteousness in the great congregation;
    behold, I did not restrain my lips;
    and that, O LORD, you know.
Your righteousness have I not hidden in my heart;
I have spoken of your faithfulness and your deliverance;
    I have not concealed your love and faithfulness from the
        great congregation.
You are the LORD;
do not withhold your compassion from me;
    let your love and your faithfulness keep me safe for ever,
For innumerable troubles have crowded upon me;
my sins have overtaken me, and I cannot see;
    they are more in number than the hairs of my head,
    and my heart fails me.
Be pleased, O LORD, to deliver me;
    O LORD, make haste to help me.

Chapter 17: A Story of Discovering God in the Neighborhood

1 Samuel 3:1–10

Now the boy Samuel was ministering to the LORD under Eli. The word of the LORD was rare in those days; visions were not widespread.

At that time Eli, whose eyesight had begun to grow dim so that he could not see, was lying down in his room; the lamp of God had not yet gone out, and Samuel was lying down in the temple of the LORD, where the ark of God was. Then the LORD called, "Samuel! Samuel!" and he said, "Here I am!" and ran to Eli, and said, "Here I am, for you called me." But he said, "I did not call; lie down again." So he went and lay down. The LORD called again, "Samuel!" Samuel got up and went to Eli, and said, "Here I am, for you called me." But he said, "I did not call, my son; lie down again." Now Samuel did not yet know the LORD, and the word of the LORD had not yet been revealed to him. The LORD called Samuel again, a third time. And he got up and went to Eli, and said, "Here I am, for you called me." Then Eli perceived that the LORD was calling the boy. Therefore Eli said to Samuel, "Go, lie down; and if he calls you, you shall say, 'Speak, LORD, for your servant is listening.'" So Samuel went and lay down in his place. Now the LORD came and stood there, calling as before, "Samuel! Samuel!" And Samuel said, "Speak, for your servant is listening."

Conclusion: Transforming the Gloom

Isaiah 55:6–11

Seek the LORD while he may be found, call upon him while he is near; let the wicked forsake their way, and the unrighteous their thoughts; let them return to the LORD, that he may have mercy on them, and to our God, for he will abundantly pardon. For my thoughts are not your thoughts, nor are your ways my ways, says the LORD. For as the heavens are higher than the earth, so are my ways higher than your ways and my thoughts than your thoughts. For as the rain and the snow come down from heaven, and do not return there until they have watered the earth, making it bring forth and sprout, giving seed to the sower and bread to the eater, so shall my word be that goes out from my mouth; it shall not return to me empty, but it shall accomplish that which I purpose, and succeed in the thing for which I sent it.